THE MUSEUM TRADING HANDBOOK

THE MUSEUM TRADING HANDBOOK

by
Hilary Blume

Published by the Charities Advisory Trust

Published by the Charities Advisory Trust, Radius Works, Back Lane, Hampstead, London NW3 1HL.

© Hilary Blume

First published 1987

Typeset by Scarborough Typesetting Services
Printed and bound in Great Britain by
Biddles Ltd, Guildford and King's Lynn

ISBN 0 907164 35 8

The research for the Museum Trading Handbook was supported by funding from the Office of Arts and Libraries.

A steering group for the project made many helpful suggestions, and the author would wish to record her thanks to Bob Harding, Richard Foster, Chris Newbery, John Fox and the staff of the Office of Arts and Libraries for their helpful comments.

The experience of members of the steering group was of great value, however the views expressed in the book are the responsibility of the author.

Contents

Introduction

Why trade?

Since the Second World War there have been enormous changes in museums in the United Kingdom. Perhaps most significant has been the enormous increase in the numbers of museums. Every local community seems intent on forming a museum, a development very often associated with saving a prominent building in the town. Every hobby and interest appears to have its own theme museum, and the increased interest in industrial archaeology coupled with the increased redundancy of our industrial buildings, has meant that many of them have been turned into museums. It has been the rise in leisure activities, and increasing mobility that have enabled people to have a day out which encompasses a museum visit.

Newly established museums, many if not most of them, dependent on a variety of sources of income as opposed to being permanently funded by local or central government, have from the beginning counted on revenue-earning as an integral part of their work. Income has come from admission fees, sale of souvenirs, catering, rents from hiring out premises, reproduction fees and even from undertaking repair work within the museums' workshops. Coupled with a need to raise funds, a need now also shared by previously statutorily funded museums, the establishment of more visitor-oriented museums, as opposed to repositories of priceless objects or sources of academic study, means that the museum shop is perceived as a service to enhance visitor enjoyment, as are the tea room and well appointed lavatories and car-parks. The new style museums also had a freshness of approach. Their collections were often very small, often with fairly commonly available objects, so that the skill of the museum was to display in such as way as to illustrate its theme (objects in context rather than objects of intrinsic value). A lack of reverence towards individual objects in its collection

1

has been very helpful in developing a museum's trading especially in their shops, because the museum's staff are not so worried about being tainted by trade, or 'cheapening' their collection by selling anything beyond academic treatises on it. Qualms about making jigsaws out of reproductions of old master paintings do not apply to jigsaws of wheelwright shops or maps of the waterways of England.

Trading by the museum, of which its shop is the most public aspect, is receiving more attention. The public are coming to expect a shop in all but the smallest museums, and coinciding as this does with the pressure on museums to generate their own funds, the increased involvement of museums in trading, and the development of museum shops seems inevitable. But running a museum shop is not so easy that success is guaranteed, indeed, people would be startled if they realised quite how many of these money-earning endeavours lost money.

Why have a shop?

The first question must be, should we have a shop, and why? And these questions should be posed whether you have a shop or not. Some museums have had shops, or sales counters, for so long that they have become a part of the fittings, and no one questions whether they should be discontinued or changed. A well run museum, or indeed any organisation, should be constantly alert to the possibilities of change. In museums where neither the collection nor its display have been changed for fifty years the existence of the postcard counter is likely to remain unchallenged, indeed almost unnoticed. The Oxford philosopher considering the proposed new shop for the Bodleian Library summed it up wonderfully 'Why is there something and not rather nothing?' This is the question that should be posed by every museum about its trading. Remember nothing is a real alternative, and may be the most profitable (if absence of loss can be considered a profit).

When asked why they had a shop, the replies of both curatorial and shop staff show a striking degree of consensus. Profit, the need for funds, was the most frequently mentioned reason, and the reason which was given top billing. The educational role of the shop, as an extension of the museum's work, was ranked as the second most important reason for having a shop. Thirdly, the shop was seen as a publicity and public relations tool, a public friendly face of the museum, which would enhance the visitors' enjoyment. A fourth, unstated reason which neither the museum directors nor shop managers would admit to, but which certainly seems to be important, is the irrational belief that having a museum shop is a sign of a dynamic, modern approach: that 'real', important museums have shops, so the shop becomes a status enhancer. A few museum directors did, with extraordinary frankness, indicate that they had shops (or sales counters) because the member of staff or volunteer had been running the shop for years and whilst it was neither profitable, nor what the museum director wanted, it was felt judicious to allow the situation to continue until old age would force retirement. This approach could be categorised as shelving the problem for 'political' reasons.

If one examines the four main reasons for having a museum shop (ignoring the political reasons) namely: 1) profit; 2) educational; 3) service to visitors and 4) as a status symbol, it is startling how few museum shops would be regarded as successful when measured against these criteria.

If one takes profit as the main criterion, it must be said that available figures suggest probably 60% of all museum shops operate at a loss, 20% break even, and possibly 20% make any sort of profit. These figures have to be viewed with care, and are admittedly only a rough estimate. Very few museum shops when accounting for their profits take into account notional rent (the premises are usually provided by the museum); staff, unless it is directly employed by the shop (usually attendants deal with counter sales as part of their warding duties); or services, such as sign posting which may also be provided by the museum, as is electricity and heating. It is astounding how many museum shops calculate their 'profits' by taking sales revenue less amount spent on stock in the current year. No account is taken of any form of overheads, nor of value of stock purchased in previous years, let alone considering the interest foregone on capital invested. A survey of museums in Yorkshire and Humberside showed that only 5% of those with a trading operation were keeping sufficient records to be able to calculate their true financial position. This ignorance of the true profitability of a museum shop is not confined to volunteer-run operations. Museum shops with turnovers of hundreds of thousands of pounds are also blissfully unaware of the true financial position of their shops. Even where a separate company has been established and one would expect the requirements of the Companies Acts would ensure proper accounts were kept, more often than not no account is taken of the services provided by the museum. It is true that one factor militating against the profitability of museum shops is that they are required to produce items such as exhibition catalogues, which are uncommercial, and profits are mopped up by this subsidy of the museum's educational publishing. But this excuse is more used than is warranted, as relatively few museums do, in fact, produce scholarly publications.

Museum shops are not very good at making profit; are they successful at extending the museum's educational programme? Some are very good at producing or stocking a wide range of material relating to their collection, at all levels of learning, from Ladybird books to academic dissertations. The shop is the specialist bookshop for the subject. They may also extend their range of goods to capitalise on the interest the visit has aroused – providing colouring books, and identification charts, inexpensive replicas, mineral samples, or scale model kits. It has been argued that the museum shop provides an open, welcoming face of the museum to the public – drawing people into a museum who might otherwise be in awe of it, and exciting their imagination once they are there. This may be true of some museum shops, but many will reinforce a feeling that the museum is a musty, old-fashioned place. People do not know how museums are run, but they are familiar with shops, and know what they look like and how they operate, and too many museum shops have a rather dismal feel about them. If museum shops are about education, then they must be attractive, lively places. They must enable the visitor to carry home with him a souvenir of the visit, which extends his knowledge, and indulges the interest the museum has stimulated.

The museum's shop can provide good or bad publicity for the museum. A well run, well-stocked shop is an attractive door to the museum, a focus of shopping for a local community, a place to find unusual gifts at a time when high street shops and department stores are increasingly, and boringly, similar. Seen as a service to the visitors some museum shops are good – the Natural History Museum does provide a wide range of inexpensive items for the many children who visit, and the National Portrait Gallery has a very good selection of items for its largely tourist visitors. Both

4

these shops cater for the sort of visitor the museum attracts, and the shops have character because of that.

The museum's shop (and tea room) is the public face of its trading. There are many other aspects of trading which the general public will not identify as trading by the museum, but may be more significant to the museum in terms of revenue. For example, licensing and other reproduction rights agreements, hire of the premises, and wholesaling products to other retail outlets. Museums are beginning to recognise the potential, and more success stories will make them want to venture into these profitable areas.

Each museum should consider what it wants out of its trading, and how best to achieve those objectives. Running a shop or tea room is likely to involve the highest over-heads (although a full blown publishing department churning out unsaleable titles is probably even more costly). They may bring the most visitor satisfaction, but may also generate the highest levels of visitor complaint. If the declared aim of the trading is to make money, it is essential that systems are set up to measure true profits. If the trading is to be run as a public relations exercise, it should be viewed, and judged, as such, and the question asked 'is it cost effective?' It might be cheaper to run a series of small ads, or a poster campaign, or employ a professional lobbyist. Look at your shop and other manifestations of your trading, and wonder what impression it gives outsiders. Look at other museums' trading and see what it can teach you. Never assume that other museums are successful at what they are doing, even when they tell you they are, because they are often unable or unwilling to make a correct assessment. Do not think that a good museum shop requires large amounts of capital investment, most museum shops would benefit from someone actually thinking about them, rather than renewing their shop fittings.

Summary

Decide why your museum should trade.

The most usual reasons are   1) profit
    2) education
    3) service to visitors
    4) status symbol

Measure your performance against these criteria.

Setting Up a Trading Company

Whatever a museum is trying to do through its trading, and whatever form that trading may take, it is important to make sure that the manner in which it trades enables it to retain any profits. It is also desirable for the museum to separate its trading function, so that the museum's main funding is not used to subsidise the running of the shop. If the trading is done through a limited company, the museum's liability for any losses the company might make is limited. In practice it would be hard for the museum to shrug off debts its trading company, clearly publicly identified with the museum, had incurred. (In theory any trustees spending charitable, i.e. museum funds, for purposes other than their principal aim, which certainly would not include trading debts, could be held to be personally liable. In practice the Charity Commissioners will give the trustees the opportunity to put their house in order.)

It is the norm, rather than the exception, for a museum administered by a local authority (and that means a substantial number of museums in the country) to have no arrangement to retain any profit earned by its trading. The money simply defrays the museum's running cost. This may seem perfectly fair to the Borough's Finance Committee, but it gives the museum little incentive to raise funds. Some museums have persuaded their local authorities that any profits from the shop may be earmarked for new acquisitions, others have managed to retain any profits for developing their trading, by being allowed to increase investment in stock, or finance improvements to the shop layout. This should only be necessary in the first few years, say up to five, after which one would expect the trading operation to have built up some working capital, but still be able to hand over some profits to the museum. More museum trading operations are now being established as separate trading companies.

6

This was essential for independent and trustee museums, where the museum was registered as a charity, because charitable status would be a limiting factor on the museum's trading.

Museums registered as charities can trade perfectly legitimately, without incurring the wrath of either the Charity Commissioners or the Inland Revenue, if their trading can be said to be in support of their educational role. Thus, if the museum shop wishes to limit itself to publications and perhaps a few postcards, it would be quite easy to argue the case for its fulfilling a purely educational role. On the other hand, it would be limiting its ability to make a profit. If the shop, as one hopes, wants to extend its range of stock into still relevant but not purely educational items such as souvenirs and gifts, then it needs to trade through a subsidiary to avoid tax on profits.

Through an extra-statutory concession the Inland Revenue will exempt from tax the profits of small-scale trading. The conditions are that the organisation is not trading regularly, that the trading is not in competition with local traders, that the trade is supported by the public because they wish to support the museum (or charity's work) and believe the profit will be applied for that work and that indeed the profits are spent for that purpose. You can in fact trade very substantially before you are likely to be challenged by the Inland Revenue. (It is rarely the Charity Commissioners who will be chasing you, unless they get a complaint, say from local traders, but rather the Inland Revenue seeking their pound of flesh.) Charities have been trading without subsidiary companies, with turnovers in excess of three million pounds, and they were not asked to pay back-tax on that trading profit, but gently advised to regularise the position by establishing a trading subsidiary. Your treatment if discovered exploiting this extra-statutory concession will depend very much on the zeal of your local tax inspector, although the Inland Revenue have been trying to ensure more consistency in applying the rules on charity trading. If you do have trouble with a tax inspector, firstly try to placate him with promises to regularise the position – 'we're planning to set up a trading company, which will covenant its profits . . .' – secondly, if he is arguing that your scale of trading is too substantial to be regarded as incidental (and a permanent shop is clearly trading regularly so you are on quite shaky ground) suggest the shop is merely pursuing the primary charitable purpose of the museum, through education. Those pencils and bookmarks with

7

your museum name on can be explained away as promotional items in support of your work. These are merely holding devices; it is really simpler, and more desirable, to regularise the position.

The standard form, preferred by the Charity Commissioners and Inland Revenue alike, is that any trading of any substance undertaken by a charity should be conducted through a limited company, which covenants any profits to the parent body, in this case the museum. The control of the company should remain rigorously in the hands of the museum, with shares in the company owned by the museum, and the directors of the company nominated by the museum (who can appoint the company's staff). The line of decision goes from staff of the trading company answerable to the company's directors (some of the museum's trustees) who are answerable to the museums governing body. The company covenants all its profits to the museum (and it could be for a specific purpose – such as new acquisitions, or refurbishment, or the maintenance of an educational programme, or at the discretion of the Director of the Board of Trustees). The wording of the covenant should be for 'all the profits'. You do not have to make a covenant for a specific sum of money. The company pays an assessed amount of Corporation Tax on its profits before the end of the financial year. The museum then re-claims the tax the company has paid from the Inland Revenue. The Inland Revenue will normally not repay the money until it receives the audited accounts of the company, because the tax paid, because it has to be done before the year end, is only an approximate amount, and it is not until the annual accounts are prepared that the exact amount will be known. New arrangements for the repayment of the tax are designed to speed up the whole process.

If the trading is run through a company it should be quite clear exactly what the income and expenditure of the shop is, and whether it is in profit or not. The Companies Acts require annual audited accounts. The auditor should make quite clear to those running the shop just what the true costs are, and take into account costs which are, in fact, being met by the museum, and at least for management accounting purposes make sure that the company recognises this subsidy. By operating through a distinct trading subsidiary one can gain a much more accurate financial picture of the whole operation, and see whether or not it is truly profitable. Having a separate trading company, with clearly measurable results, also stimulates the staff, making them more involved in achieving better results. Their performance becomes more easily measurable. They also feel loyalty to the more easily recognisable team that they and their colleagues in the trading company form.

To form a trading subsidiary you need a solicitor who has a knowledge of charity law. There are, in fact, law practices specializing in charity law. The whole process should be very simple and straightforward. The basic rules are that the raising of money for charity, whether by trading or any other means, is not in itself a charitable activity. A charity has to be established for charitable purposes only; even if only one of its purposes were deemed not to be charitable then the organisation as a whole would not be able to register as a charity. Any organisation which states amongst its aims the carrying out of trade (in any form, and however stated) would not be able to register as a charity. This does not mean that a charity cannot trade, but that it must not be set up to do so as its prime aim, but merely as an ancillary activity to raise funds to support its main work. To do this, a charity's trust deed must give it the power to trade. If, for whatever reason, and it may simply be bad legal draftsmanship, the charity is not empowered to trade by its trust deed then that is an end to the matter. Nor may a charity trade via a trading subsidiary owned by itself where its trustees have no power to make this kind of investment. It is very important when drawing up a charity's trust deed that the trustees' powers are very wide, so that they can deal with changing circumstances.

A problem area for a charity's trading company is that it has to pay over to the charity, before the end of its financial year, any profits. This means that the company cannot retain funds to invest in increased stock or build up any reserve; in other words it is starved of working capital. This is overcome by the company borrowing from the museum at the beginning of each year to fund its stock purchases, and possibly running costs (if it is the slack time of the year). The money should be lent at commercial rates of interest. It is very galling to those running trading subsidiaries of charities, whether the charity is a museum or otherwise, to have to go cap-in-hand with their budget and ask for funding for their company, when they have just handed over their profits, which are hopefully more than they are borrowing. If the relationship between the museum and the company is close, and there is agreement over the running of the company then it should not be a time of friction

9

or humiliation. As the trading company expands it may find that its actual profits are reduced because of the cost of borrowing at commercial rates. It is tactful for the parent charity to acknowledge this, and add on to the profits the interest payments (or part of them) when calculating the real profits earned by the shop. This combined figure is, of course, unofficial, but may encourage the trading company, whose performance is being penalised by the requirements of charity law. The position might also warrant a note in the accounts!

If a museum is not a registered charity, for example, if it is administered by the local authority, then it has to follow a slightly different procedure if it is to form a trading company, and avoid paying tax on its trading profits, because only a registered charity is able to reclaim the tax on covenants made for charitable purposes. It is still desirable for a museum to separate its trading from its main activity, because it imposes financial control on the operation, and stops the museum unwittingly subsidising its trading. It also avoids the tax liability, which for even a small scale operation probably means about 30% of its profits. The museum may, in fact, have a mechanism it could use to channel its trading profits through, for example, a Friends Association which is registered as a charity. If the museum has no related body with charitable status, it could set up either a Friends of the 'X' Museum, or if the Director does not want a Friends Group, and the trouble of supporters, a simple X Museum Trust, whose charitable objects would be to support the Museum in its educational role, and in its work to benefit the Community. Remember you will not get registration if you state the purpose is to raise funds for 'X' Museum, because fund-raising, like trading, is not a charitable purpose, it is merely a power, and should be in the trust deed as such. It is sensible for a museum to have a charitable arm, not just to receive profits from its trading and recover tax, but to safeguard income donated to the museum, and make sure it does not end up in the local authority budget, but brings additional benefit to the museum, beyond its usual local authority funding. It would avoid the scandalous situation now often prevalent, where the donations collected at the museum ostensibly for its work, are simply emptied into the local authority coffers.

One disincentive against setting up a trading company is that the company will not be entitled to rate relief (the current legislation provides for a 50% mandatory rate relief, and 50% at the discretion of the local authority for registered charities). A trading company is not entitled to rate relief, and rates may be levied on that proportion of the museum's premises used by the trading company, not just the shop but any storage and administrative offices. In practice, a museum not registered as a charity, say in local authority management, will be exempt from rates (the Rating Authority will make a book entry only) but its trading may not be exempt. A great deal depends on the attitude of the local rating officers. Some, if not most, will turn a blind eye to any museum trading. Others are very zealous and will exact every last half-penny out of the trading company. They feel completely justified to do so, because they argue that their job is to collect rates, which are used for the general good. If the museum's trading company is exempt from rates, they argue it is unfair competition to local traders. It is, indeed, very often complaints by local traders which precipitate the visit of the rating officer, most often it seems when the museum opens a tea room, actual shops seem to go largely unnoticed.

In almost all cases it is better to pay any rates, or taxes, and develop the trading to its full potential rather than restrict your trading in the hope of avoiding attention.

Summary

It is best to set up a trading subsidiary through which to conduct the museum's trading. The preferred form is a limited company owned and controlled by the museum through the appointment of its directors. The company covenants all profits to the museum, or a charity to benefit the museum.

The Educational Role of Trading

Years before the museum shop developed as a source of souvenirs, museums have seen the production of publications about their collections, both catalogues and monographs by the curatorial staff, as an important and essential part of their work. Whilst the museum shop is sometimes regarded, like a tea room, as a not altogether essential visitor amenity, there is virtually no museum which would want to eschew what can be called 'academic publishing'. The museum's scholarly publications are seen as an enhancement and validation of the museum's role as an educational institution, disseminating knowledge.

Funding the scholarly publications, with their inevitably restricted market, has been a perennial problem for all galleries and museums. If a simple 'everything has to cover costs' rule were applied to these publications then there would be no hope of the detailed catalogue or scholarly monograph ever being produced. The museum would scarcely produce anything more learned than a general guidebook! Many museums have seen the development of their trading companies and shops as a way of earning the funds to subsidise their scholarly publications. Thus, the Director of the British Museum, Sir David Wilson, in a speech at the Stationers Hall in May 1982, described the Museum's trading subsidiary: 'It is entirely self-supporting, the profits going towards the publication of the learned output of the staff. . . . The sale of exhibition catalogues, of guides, replicas and jewellery; of games, postcards and slides, has enabled us to publish some five or six learned catalogues each year. Hefty, enduring works of scholarship which will stand for years as major academic sources . . . Primarily, the British Museum is a place of scholarship.'

It is important if the trading company is expected to subsidise publications that everyone understands this. It is unfair to castigate the trading company for failing to make profits when it is having to sink those profits into subsidy of non-commercial publishing. For internal accounting purposes it is sensible for the trading company to list the level of subsidy it is making to the museum for 'educational purposes'; this gives a more accurate picture of the trading company's true profitability.

It is very usual for charities when their fund-raising goes awry to say the event, or whatever, was for public relations, not fund-raising. Similarly, one hears often from museum trading companies with badly run shops that the shop has an educational function. They mean, presumably, that the trading company is subsidising non-commercial publishing, stocking esoteric scholarly items with slow sales, and producing at a loss material for children to help them understand the musuem. One can think of no museum trading company in the UK which is running at a loss because of its educational work, though one can think of many examples of where it is used as an excuse for poor performance. Having subsidy quantified in the management accounts should make it easier for the museum's and trading company's management to judge the validity of the excuses.

As with every other aspect of its work the museum trading company must have a plan, setting out its educational objects and how it hopes to achieve them, with a budget. Overleaf is a simple educational publishing plan for an imaginary museum. It is recently opened and has no back-stock except a few black and white postcards!

From our example you see that the museum is going to produce as quickly as possible trail sheets and a Teachers Pack for school visits. Teachers will be encouraged to buy the pack ahead of time, so they can plan the visit, and prepare the children for it. The museum will take care to have the Teachers Pack on sale in the shop so parents with a didactic disposition can buy it! The production of the Pack and Trail Sheets is inexpensive − it can be produced at the local 'copy shop', taking advantage of new technology! A guide book is seen as an important publication; depending on the budget it can be a full colour booklet or an A4 2-fold leaflet. The time it will take to produce the booklet means it will probably be sensible in the interim, to produce a simple leaflet as soon as possible, this should be a matter of a few hundred pounds, so is easy enough to accommodate in the

Educational Programme – Museum Shop – stock only (not lectures etc.)

Target Customer	Item	Source	Funding for items
School children	Trail sheet	Own production	Inexpensive – own fund
	Quiz sheet		Inexpensive – own fund
	Colouring books	Specialist suppliers/	Buy in from other suppliers
	Models	other museums	unless have sufficient
	Books		capital
	(Material to be divided		
	– primary, secondary		
	school, university)		
Teachers	Trail sheet & quizzes	Own publications	Inexpensive – own fund
	(with answers)		
	Theme & activity sheets		Inexpensive – own fund
	Guide book		Expensive – either go to
			specialist publishers
			(see p. 52) needing no
			capital or seek sponsorship)
	Notes for teachers on		Inexpensive – own fund
	school visits (Museum		
	School Pack)		
	Books of general interest	Other publishers	See note above
Interested amateurs	Guide book	Own publication	Own funds, seek
	Catalogues to special	Own publication	sponsorship
	exhibitions		Ambitious – seek sponsorship
	Museum Journal	Own publication	Order as able
	Books on subject of	Other publishers	
	museum's collection		
All visitors	Postcards – of few	Own publication	Postcards tie up capital
	items in collection	Other museums if	– be cautious
		related items	

budget. In the meantime either a sponsor could be found to pay for the guide book, or a deal could be struck with a commercial publisher (see p. 52)

There is a wide range of books available from publishers that relate to the museum's collection, not least of all those produced by other museums. The budget must allow for the purchase of some stock (some publishers have sale or return arrangements and these will be taken advantage of – though not too rigorously or publishers may refuse to supply in future!) and exchange deals can be struck with other museums. Other museums too will be a rich source of other educational material such as colouring sheets, model kits and games.

As the stock builds up, and income is generated through sales, the museum shop can develop and expand its publishing programme. Consultation with the curatorial staff should make it possible to draw up a schedule of catalogues for special exhibitions. There is nothing virtuous about the crisis management that is favoured by some museum publications departments where, for example, exhibition catalogues are received from the printer by express delivery minutes before the private view. (This is inevitably a very expensive way of operating – if you are always behindhand it is certain that you will be forced to pay more for production, because you are choosing a typesetter, designer, printer and binder not on price, or even on quality, but because they can do the work quickly). If you work to a plan then you can make sure the manuscript is available on schedule and you will have gone out to competitive tender on the printing. The more business-like approach will also bring forth better performance from those responsible for producing the work on time – if you are seen as always in a flap, chasing one missed deadline after the other, then no-one will take your schedules seriously and you will always be kept waiting for texts, for photographs, or any other component for which the museum staff are responsible.

When you are producing educational material consider first who is the user. If it is for children write it simply. If it is for the general reader make it interesting but not too specialised. Not every date and name has to be listed in the text. It is more important that the reader's interest is sustained, and that the information is set in context, than that the publication lists every known fact. Any publication sold by a museum has to be accurate, but do not get obsessive, and ban every publication because the curator thinks the author's interpretation misleading! (There are some museums where the shops are allowed nothing except a few scholarly journals, because the heads of certain departments condemn every popular work on their subject.) If you have problems with curatorial interference, ask that member of staff to nominate ten publications which will suit children and the generally interested visitor — they will probably, having been consulted, choose the same books as you — because in an imperfect world you have to settle for something!

It may be useful to visitors for you to produce, and sell, bibliographies on various topics, say Roman Britain or Local History. You could charge a token 10 or 25p for the list. You may produce a fact sheet on other collections in the area. Do not underestimate the need in our examination conscious society for reading lists, and easy access information — this is an area that museum shops have scarcely touched on.

Make sure your educational material, such as trail sheets, are on display near the entrance to the museum. It is surprising how many museums do not even display trail sheets in their shop, let alone by the entrance, where most likely interested customers would find them. It is an education in itself to ask at the information desk whether there are trail sheets available. Often one is directed to the Education Offices (three doors away down a corridor in the basement and across the courtyard . . .) and can uncover the trail only with extreme determination. Encourage parents to use trail sheets in conjunction with their visits, by promoting their sale, and lending (or selling) pencils, and erasers and clip boards. If you have trail sheets for particular exhibitions tell the public about them. Remember, educational material is not to improve the compiler's education!

Summary

Generally museums like to publish scholarly works, and are only inhibited by a lack of funds. They are not always so keen to produce and stock educational material of a less academic nature. If the museum is to fulfil its educational role, it must have suitable material for a broad range of visitors.

Style

The most successful shops are those that have a consistency of style. This is true not just of museum shops, but of all retail enterprises from Marks and Spencer to Sainsburys. Similarly, a key reason for the decline of retailers such as Woolworths and Debenhams has been their failure to achieve a consistency of style which showed itself in its marketing and merchandise, so there was no particular constituency for those shops. Consistency of style can be clearly seen in shops such as Laura Ashley and Habitat and it is interesting that retailers are deliberately establishing chains of shops, not allowing them to develop and expand but pre-planning them, on the basis of their appeal to a particular sector of the market, which is catered for not just by the stock but by the style of the shop — its display, even the choice of background music. The Next and Now chains are supreme examples of this type of 'theme' merchandising.

These shops are a long way from museum trading, with the post-card counter, and the museum attendant acting as part-time sales assistant, but they do contain a very important lesson for anyone concerned with trading. Identify your customers — and cater for them not only by offering them things they want to buy but enabling them to do so in a manner and setting that they find pleasant. The tone you set should be reflected in every aspect of your shop — from staff to display.

What style are you going to adopt? What type of person do you want to attract into the shop, who will feel at ease in it, and like the experience? The first thing is to make sure that those running the museum and those running the trading company agree on the style of the shop. You can save yourself a great deal of criticism if you all agree from the first what type of shop the museum shop will be. Firstly, you must all agree as to what market the shop will cater for. You need to think about who visits the museum. You will almost certainly have schoolchildren —some en masse with their teachers,

17

others with parents. You may have tourists — back-packers on limited budgets, or more affluent visitors. Perhaps your museum attracts the enthusiasts and scholars. Probably, some from each category will be amongst your visitors. You have to decide which group you want to aim to attract in the shop.

It is possible to try to cater for all possible types of customer, but the chance of doing so satisfactorily is slight. The shop will look too disjointed — it will lack an overall 'look' or 'style' so it will not be attractive to any one group and this will be reflected in low sales. One way of overcoming this is, where practical, to divide the shop into a 'children's corner', a book-browsing section and so on. At Quarry Bank Mill the bar is turned into a temporary children's shop during the day, to overcome the problem of swarms of children destroying the shopping 'experience' for their higher-spending elders. The Natural History Museum has, in effect, a children's shop, physically separated from the main gift shop, which again is separated from the bookshop.

Apart from deciding on the style of the shop on the basis of its likely 'constituency' you also have to consider what shop the museum wants. Very few museum staff want a shop that looks like a tacky souvenir shop (and it is therefore surprising how many of them do look just that). This shows how without thinking about it, by not setting a style on the shop, the stock imposes its own style. Most museums, when asked, would like their museum shops to be a cross between a bookshop and a Design Centre style gift shop, with a children's section of low price souvenir items in a strategically safe place. These are perfectly achievable aims, as long as one keeps them to the forefront. As well as the museum's view of what type of shop it wants, there is a certain duty to provide visitors with a shop which at least approximates to their expectations, and desires — to take an extreme and foolish example to illustrate the point, visitors would be surprised, and unlikely to buy, if they found the museum shop sold nothing but electrical fittings or plumbing materials. Put at its simplest the museum shop has to be recognisable to its potential customers as a museum shop — both by virtue of its stock, and its appearance — a shop has to look like a shop if people are to respond to it as a shop, and buy things at it.

Though striving for a style for your shop do not over-dress it. You do not want your customers to feel guilty about handling goods because they are disturbing your display! You do not want them to feel that the image you have created could not be replicated by them in their own homes. Do not make your shop such a stage set that the customer views it merely as an extension of the museum. For example, the American Museum at Claverton Manor has as its shop a reconstructed country store. The shelves are filled with period goods. More than two-thirds of the items on display are old and not for sale. The goods that are for sale are, of course, very disappointing by comparison, so the customer is deterred from buying by the setting, rather than encouraged by it. The shop detracts from its merchandise. One feels much more comfortable buying the splendid home-baked cookies in the neutral atmosphere of the tea room.

Your choice of stock will reflect your taste. However much you believe that you are buying what you judge will sell, rather than what you would buy for yourself, remember it is your perception of other people's taste that all the goods are filtered through. It is a great virtue in any shop for stock to be 'selected with a single eye' – as the marketing jargon has it. This concept is difficult to explain, though not hard to understand intuitively. It can go disastrously wrong, if the person making the selection is completely out of tune with the potential customers, but generally it will seem that the unity and consistency of style will appeal to a sector, which will buy well, rather than the mish-mash of stock which pleases no one. Fortunately, in retailing you have a very efficient way of testing your mistakes; if it works it sells – if it does not you have unsold stock. So the retailer can usually tell if the 'style' he is setting is the right one for the market. It is important to realise that you will not expect to please all sectors under this policy of consistency of style – but you will maximise profits by pleasing a large enough market, who will buy more substantially from you than they would in a shop with no distinct character. Looked at another way, the museum shop extends the visitors' experience of the museum, and caters for his wishes and expectations for that visit.

The National Trust shops in England and Wales give us perhaps the widest known illustration of the heritage shop which follows a distinct style – and tries, not always equally successfully, but sometimes supremely well, to suggest to the customer that some of the experience of country house living can be taken home and enjoyed by purchase of National Trust polish, toiletries and foods, packed in nostalgic style with nostalgic names. These products become real souvenirs of the visit.

The Royal Academy is a very interesting example of museum trading done with consistency of style. The range of products produced specially for the RA may seem awesomely expensive to those unused to shopping on Sloane Street, but they form a very distinctive range, which appeals not so much to the casual visitor to the shop who is unlikely to make a £30 or £40 unplanned purchase but to a regular clientele. There seems little doubt that many visitors to the RA may find the items in the shop beyond their means, though there are a few relatively inexpensive items, and many may find them too well designed and not tacky enough – but how splendid of the RA to have the courage of its convictions and produce a range of well designed 'upmarket' items. The RA has built up a reputation for its products, and is attracting customers who visit the shop to buy presents, for example, though not visiting the exhibitions. People coming to the shop, not the gallery, are a success in trading if not in museum terms!

In fact, in both the National Trust and Royal Academy shop, much, if not most of the stock, is similar, if not identical, to that stocked by other museum shops. But it is by having a prominently displayed selection of specially commissioned items that in fact the whole stock seems new and unusual. Behavioural studies on shopping habits show that customers associate a shop with items that are less than 5% of its total range.

In both the National Trust and the RA shop people know what to expect. They come not necessarily to buy a specific item, but because they know the type of things they can find there. In a world of increasing sameness in shops (where Selfridges and Harrods have much the same stock) it is the strength of a museum shop that it can be a source of unusual, distinctive items, not generally available. The museum shop that builds up its reputation as a source of a particular type of product will benefit enormously. It does not matter if it is for up-market gifts like the Royal Academy, or the ideal £2–£3 Christmas present for an aunt like The National Trust, what matters is that you will build up a loyal group of customers, who will come and buy again and again – and they are of more value than the visitor to the museum who may never return.

Virtually all the successful museum shops, if not all, have a distinct style. In some cases they have built up a reputation as a place in which to shop for specific items – the Bodleian Library in Oxford is known as a good source of Christmas cards; the Fitzwilliam Museum has a strong selection of art books. These shops cater very much for local people, who will visit the shop for specific items. An interesting aspect of shopping habits is that distance travelled is more important than the time spent in the shop in determining the value of a transaction. This means that if someone makes a special journey to your museum shop, as opposed to your museum, they are likely to spend more. Successful shops, such as the National Portrait Gallery, will cater for the tourist and manage to provide a serious alternative to the Piccadilly Circus souvenir stall. This shop, without very grand stock, offers a soothing and restrained atmosphere in keeping with the Gallery. It is a good illustration of the fact that the style of a shop can be set not by its stock, but by the layout, the staff and the indefinable 'atmosphere' of the place.

Whatever the museum, and whatever its shop, it should be possible for the customer to be taken blindfold into the shop and still recognise firstly, that he is in a museum shop, and secondly, without reading the names on the key fobs, to know what that museum's collection is about. It is surprising how many museum shops, if not approached through the museum, so immediately set in context, would tell the customer nothing about the museum. Their stock does not relate to anything much − nor does the 'feel' of the shop make it seem an extension of the museum. The stock appears to be on offer because those running the shop either over-ordered, so have an apparently endless supply, for example, of black and white postcards, or because some manufacturer has off-loaded his special offers. The prize for inappropriate stock should perhaps be offered to the National Gallery for its pile of remaindered books, including a Children's Bible with lurid 1950's style illustrations.

An American, Joseph Weishar, has observed that 'successful retailers merchandise their wares so that products and services are in keeping with the preconception of the prospective buyers', highlighting the fact that customers want to buy in the right places − as the jargon has it 'peer status in ownership is equalled by the status of shopping in the right places'. Customers like to purchase products in stores that they would not be ashamed to be seen buying in by friends. These statements may seem far fetched, but consider, if one were doing one's Christmas shopping for a large number of family and friends, wanting to buy something they will like, but perhaps equally hoping to find something that looks like it cost more than it did, would one feel better about being observed by friends shopping for gifts in Harrods than in a temporary shop selling bankrupt stock at knock-down prices! Snobbish, yes; less than frank and open, yes; human, yes.

A shop should reflect the enthusiasm of its staff for the products they are selling, and in a museum, for the subject of the collection. The visitor's enthusiasm for what he has seen in the museum should be increased by his visit to the shop – because it is in the shop that the information can be made accessible to him at home – he cannot take home a Roman mosaic, but he can take a picture of one, a book about Roman mosaics, perhaps even a tapestry kit to combine both the pleasure of sewing with a souvenir of the visit. The purchase he can make in the shop can remind him of the pleasure he had in the visit. It can offer him an opportunity to extend his knowledge, and to discuss with other enthusiasts (hopefully the shop staff) the rival merits of one book on the subject compared with another. Marshal McLuhan had a message for those in museum trading, it may be un-welcome but it is there – the material available in the shop is more real to the average visitor than the objects in the museum. That being the case, it is clearly important for the shop to be an extension of the museum, in its style and content.

Summary

A museum shop should, through its stock, its display and its staff, strive for a consistency of style. This style will determine its market, so should be appropriate to actual visitors. The most successful museum and gallery shops are those which manage to achieve a distinctive 'personality'.

What To Sell and Where To Get It

Your stock, the goods you are offering for sale, is what is going to earn you money. However beautiful your shop, however well sign-posted and lit, however friendly and courteous your staff, your shop cannot succeed if the goods on sale are, of themselves, unattractive to the customer.

Establishing criteria for stock

You should, to overcome subsequent disagreement, and to increase the chance of the shop having a style or identity which is likely to improve its performance, set out criteria for selecting stock. The list may go something like this:

1. Relevance
   Goods must be relevant to the museum's collection
   or to the geographical area
   or of general educational interest
   or appropriate to the museum

2. Profitability
   Items should not be deliberately stocked at a loss except when judged to be of over-riding educational or scholarly importance.

3. Origin of manufacture
   Goods should be made in the UK except where no similar UK made goods are available (publications excepted).
   A proportion should foster local, traditional crafts.
   A proportion should foster artistic excellence.

23

4. Publications

   The curatorial staff may reserve the right to veto, on scholarly grounds, the stock of certain publications (this power of veto must be used sparingly).

5. The quality of reproductions of works of art must be to a standard consistent with the museum's reputation.

6. Replicas

   All replicas must be marked as such.

7. The museum's good name must not be jeopardised by the design or quality of the goods offered in its shops, and the short term profitability of the shop should not be set above its duty to the museum.

These criteria outline the main areas in which policy could usefully be set out. Ideally once the rules have been set out the head of the trading company will be allowed to get on with his job, without interference. The rules exist as a guideline for him, and as a tool should the trading company's management find it to be necessary to check his activities. It is good that people agree what sort of shop they want, and what sort of goods they want in that shop. Within the broad, agreed criteria, it is up to the head of trading to make that decision, and you have to be careful that inviting people to be party to drawing up the criteria does not give them a licence to interfere, or carp, subsequently.

The criteria you establish are not holy writ. You may find them unworkable. Your shop may be full of beautiful, hand-crafted items for which you do not have the market, and cannot realistically foster one in your locality. In that case you have to re-examine whether your criterion (to benefit artist craftsmen) is realisable. You may want, above all, to support a publishing venture for the museum, which as its main criterion declares that the works of the curatorial staff of the museum have an automatic right of publication. This may have been a viable proposition when the criterion was established, because the museum's director was a latter-day Sir Mortimer Wheeler, with two television series running concurrently. A change of Director would radically change the situation. A re-examination of the whole trading enterprise would become necessary.

The criteria should not be used to justify poor performance. For example 'We cannot hope to make a profit because we are not allowed to stock anything that would be popular'. If you find that the criteria are being used to justify poor performance it should sound alarm bells in your head. Either the complainant is justified, or partially, and the criteria should be re-examined, or they should be told to stop complaining and accept responsibility for the poor performance.

Stock turn and value of stock

You must have enough stock to be able to generate sales at a sufficient level to cover your overheads. Many museum shops just do not have enough on sale to make their enterprise viable, for if they sold all their stock in a relatively short period the sales income would still not cover the running costs of the shop. It is a very useful exercise, and one that should be repeated at least quarterly to calculate the total retail value of the stock – at full price. Then make a realistic adjustment, firstly by removing unsaleable items, or at least calculating how many you might expect to sell in the period. For example, the retail value of exhibition catalogues of past exhibitions may be £3,500, but you may, in a three month period only expect to sell 20 copies at £2 each. Similarly, the value of all postcards at retail value may be £20,000 but you may only expect to sell £4,000–worth in the three month period. Once you have made a list of firstly, stock value by selling price, adjusted for realistic sales levels, you may find you are projecting sales of a dismal £10,000 value, which is £2,000 less than you need to cover overheads. Things are not as bad as they seem! You have not taken into account the fact that some items, such as film, or button badges, are such fast sellers that you will have to re-order them during the period, possibly as often as once a month. (They are stock items, available within 3 days of re-order, so you can afford not to hold large quantities of stock!)

The speed with which an item sells is called its stock-turn, and this is a way of measuring the performance of various items. Retailers aim to reach or surpass certain 'stock-turn' norms for their particular type of shop. Museum shops would expect a lower stock-turn performance than either a bookshop or a gift shop, but over-all a busy museum with a large number of visitors should probably be aiming at an annual stock-turn of 3, and be quite pleased if they achieve 2. Some items will achieve a better stock-turn than others – film (for visitors' cameras) can reach a 6-turn; jewellery and gift items 4-turn and printed goods, such as publications will be poor performers at less than 1½-turn. To improve your stock-turn, increase the space you give to fast-selling items and try to reduce investment in the slow sellers. Of course, you cannot always pick a winner, and you will have items that perform better or worse than predicted, but try to identify fast sellers, and restrict investment in slow moving stock, because it is tying up capital.

In your trading you should be constantly trying to increase your sales with less investment in stock. You must have a fast stock-turn to keep your cash flow healthy – and not keep your capital tied up in stock (remember with inflation and loss of interest earnings capital can cost you about 15% a year). The best ways of improving stock-turn are to plan your buying; to keep your number of lines down; to keep accurate records of stock levels, so you do not re-order too quickly; to arrange delivery close to the time when you will sell the goods, so you do not tie up cash in stock too early; try to arrange good credit terms from suppliers, which will help cash flow; and try to speed the sales of slow selling stock by quick, effective price cuts, of at least 25%; and lastly, be very careful about buying items for special, short-term exhibitions, because once the exhibition is over these goods become as interesting as yesterday's newspapers!

Buying stock

Museum shops are largely derivative in what they stock – that is, they stock what other museum shops stock because they think they have to, the customers will expect it, so, for example, virtually every museum shop will have postcards. Museum shops often carry the same stock, for example, leather bookmarks, because the manufacturer will be assiduous in sending a sales 'rep' to call on the museum's shop manager, who is too hard-pressed to get out to find stock for himself. Like a 19th century farmer's wife relying on the local pedlar, the shop manager's choice is restricted to what is brought to him. And finally museum shops often have little variety of stock, and what they have is a poorly balanced selection, because their capital is tied up in too few items – so the scholarly catalogue of the collection may sell 20 copies a year, and have eaten up the year's purchasing budget. These are the three over-riding factors in explaining why museum shops generally look the way they do, and should form the basis of three rules of how not to buy stock for a shop.

Firstly, draw up a list of the items you think your museum shop should offer. Against each item on that list, note whom you think the article would be bought by, and why your shop should stock it. (For example, item: trail sheet, target customer: children, parents for children, teachers for children.) Then add to that list (which could become your shopping list for stock) ideas for possible sources for those goods – a manufacturer, if you know one, or another museum, or a note to ask another museum shop where they get similar products. Then take the third factor into consideration, which is that you must not tie up too much capital into any one item, or else you will not be able to buy a balanced range. Jot down against each item how much of your budget for stock purchase you want to spend on any one product. It might be useful to do this in terms of the percentage of the total budget. This particular calculation is very important, because it forces you to relinquish products which may be nearest to your heart, but you simply cannot afford. If you spread your capital over a range of products, rather than invest it in one item (most usually a slow selling publication!) you increase your chances of accumulating enough capital to make a more substantial investment in goods later.

Plan your buying of stock at least six months in advance. You will have to give it some thought substantially ahead of time, because you will have had to have fixed purchase levels in your budget. How do you know how much to order (assuming you have decided, roughly, the type of goods you want to stock)? Your stock levels do, of course, have to relate to what you expect to sell. You do not need £1 million of stock if your last year's turnover was £25,000! Usually your clearest indication of what level of stock you should have (both overall, and of any one item) is last year's sales plus any trend showing an increase in visitors since then plus expected increases caused by special exhibitions. Offset against these any likely downward trends caused by adverse conditions such as re-building of the museum, lack of special exhibitions or change in public holiday dates, which may shorten the season.

You need sales of a certain level to generate enough income to cover all overheads, pay for stock and make a profit. These figures will be included in your annual budget (and your management accounts will monitor performance). You must order your stock to fit in with your cash flow (see p. 87) so that your stock levels are at their lowest at the quietest times of the year. Remember when ordering that different items will have different delivery schedules. Some may be stock items, available virtually on demand, others may take weeks to arrive. You must know the re-order time for each item, so that you know when to re-order. This is particularly important on fast-selling lines. If the re-order time is long then you have good reason to order in substantial quantities, even though you are tying up capital. You can always ask the manufacturer to stagger delivery, and therefore payment, throughout the season.

Try to increase your profit margins by asking the supplier for a better price, for carriage free delivery, for better terms of payment (for example 60 days to pay) for a discount for payment within 14 days, for a discount for quantity, for promotional material or display copies, and even sale or return arrangements. Try to build up a good working relationship with your suppliers, and identify profitable manufacturers, as well as items. Often a supplier of a good selling item will in fact have other good selling lines, because the style of product is right for your customers.

Apart from the travelling salesmen, with their suitcases full of trinkets on which they can print your logo, (and they find you, you do not have to seek them out) where do you find suppliers? The first port of call should be other museum shops. See what they stock, and who supplies it. Generally, the manufacturer's name will be found on an item, if not ask the museum shop manager – ask him too if he would recommend the manufacturer, and if there are any problems, like minimum orders, or unreliability. There may be items that are produced by other museums that you could stock – usually the museum is only too happy to supply to other outlets. Make sure you ask for trade terms. You probably cannot visit every museum shop to discover what goods they produce you may want to stock, so you can write to those with similar collections, to ask if they have any relevant products for sale, or you can visit the annual trade show mounted by the Group for Museum Publishing and Shop Management at the Arts Council, a very modest affair, but one at which about 20 museums and others show what they have available. The MUSPUB Fair is specifically for museums. There are a whole series of trade shows in the UK that may be relevant to those stocking the museum shop.

For gifts, the major show is the Spring Fair held in the first week in February (Sunday to Thursday) at the National Exhibition Centre, Birmingham. This is a daunting event, with literally thousands of companies exhibiting their ranges of goods. The show is divided into 5 halls. The most relevant to museum shops are probably the stationery hall and the huge general gift hall, where you can find everything from trinket boxes to umbrella stands. If your time is limited then it is probably sensible to concentrate on the Design Centre display, which is always full of new ideas, and usually relatively inexpensive items. At all Trade Fairs, but most of all at Birmingham because of its size, wear comfortable shoes, because you will walk miles up and down the aisles. (The phrase 'museum feet' takes on new meaning at the Spring Show.) Also take plenty of visiting cards, as all suppliers will ask where you are from, and view with suspicion anyone unable to supply a card. You will also need to show your credentials to be admitted to the shows, as they are restricted to trade only.

The Harrogate Gift Fair in July is a smaller, friendlier show than Birmingham, thought by some to be stronger on craft items. The 'Top Drawer Show' is a much smaller, more manageable show – with 250 exhibitors of 'up market' gift-ware and stationery, and is held in September in London. Which show you choose to concentrate on will depend on proximity to the exhibition site, and your availability at the time of exhibition. Some shows are likely to have more relevant items than others. As well as the main gift shows you may also want to visit the Souvenir Show held in London at the end of October at which about 50 major souvenir manufacturers exhibit. The Premiums Show in London in the autumn may be worth a visit – it overlaps somewhat with the Souvenir Show. There is a new trade show for greetings cards – Profitable Greetings held at Brighton in September. The Booksellers Association Trade Exhibition in Brighton, in May, has not just books on display but also shop display systems and design and printing services. The London Book Fair held in London in May is a good place to see what publishers have on offer. To find out which trade fairs are to be held when and where you can consult the Trade Promotions Guide issued by the Fairs and Promotions Branch of the Department of Trade.

When you go to a Trade Show you do not have to order then and there. In fact it makes sense to leave ordering till you get back to the office, because in the heady atmosphere of the Show it is easier to over-order. Some manufacturers may have 'show specials', discounts if you order then and there. Ask if you can have the show special price if you order within 14 days. It is the job of those exhibiting at the shows to sell. They may be very persuasive, and flatter you by suggesting that such a marvellous museum shop will attract hordes of visitors, and therefore have no trouble in selling 5 gross of their special new line. By sticking to a policy of placing no orders at the show, you are less likely to be persuaded into over-ordering. Remember, you must stick to your budget! Make sure you collect information on products you like. Ask the manufacturer for samples (and expect to pay for them).

It is important to visit trade shows because it will show you what is available. It will help you to know what the trends are in giftware, and also enable you to establish a relationship with new suppliers, and keep in touch with old ones. The goods you see may also give you fresh ideas on products you might originate yourself, and even on ways to display them.

You do not have to go to all the Trade Shows. When judging which to go to, weigh up the expense, the time lost away from the shop or office, against the expected benefit. If you have a purchasing budget of £10,000, only one third of which is going to be spent on gift items, then it is unrealistic to spend three days at the Spring Show in Birmingham. It is crucial to get out and see what is going on beyond your own museum – in other museums, in other shops and to see the trends as shown at trade shows. Do not concentrate just on trade shows, because many small, local suppliers cannot afford the many thousands of pounds it costs to exhibit at them. If you only buy at trade shows your shop will be like everyone else's. Your success depends on your ability to seek out, or initiate unusual items.

Developing your own products

One way of ensuring that you can offer items that fit in to your stock-purchase criteria is to develop your own products. Your ability to do so will depend on the availability of funds, because apart from the cost of manufacture (and almost inevitably you will have to buy substantial quantities to buy at a low enough unit cost) you have to fund the development costs (your time and the cost of design). The advantage of offering your products for sale are, firstly, the relevance to your collection; secondly, its exclusivity – it is not an item to be found elsewhere; thirdly, hopefully, it is an attractive item tailored to your market; fourthly, the profitability may well be greater. The disadvantages are firstly, that you are tying up capital, secondly, that you have to order in substantial quantities, thus slowing your stock-turn and worsening your cash flow, and thirdly, you are taking a risk, as the product may fail to sell (with bought-in products your risk is limited as you order less, also the product has a track record you can enquire into).

Own products can be divided into those that follow a formula, and whilst they are peculiar to the particular museum, for example, by having the logo or name on, follow an established format. Postcards, bookmarks and pens and pencils all fall within this category. There are specialist manufacturers, and the museum does little beyond supplying a 'house style' name or suitable picture. You can be more ambitious and commission David Gentleman to design a logo for you (as did the Bodleian Library) but for most museums and galleries the design input is minimal. These type of items have fairly standard profit margins, usually around the 100% mark-up general in the gift trade, and the manufacturer will often have a suggested retail price. These are the lowest risk 'own products' because there is, in fact, very little new about them. Your risk is simply that you have to order more at a time than you may of other bought in items.

Between the full blown new product you develop completely, and the souvenir items that are personalised by having the museum's name on, there is a continuum of products which can be bought 'off the peg', with your image incorporated, such as tea towels or aprons, through to products which you originate both in form and decoration. Tea-towels, aprons, shopping bags (full-scale and in children's sizes) are all basic items on which you can have any image imposed. You may choose a picture or object from your collection, old wallpaper design, or old advertisement, selecting both on intrinsic attractiveness of the image, and whether it will reproduce well. You may limit your selection to items you feel would not be debased by being so used, for example, a Michaelangelo madonna would be rather tasteless on a tea-towel, whereas an early Sunlight Soap advertisement would seem appropriate.

31

When you are considering developing your own products firstly look at what other museums sell, and see if you could produce a similar item for your museum (for example, a cookery book, an engagement diary, an address book, a tote bag.) Do you have anything in your collection that you could reproduce – not perhaps as a straight replica, but adapt. Could a collection of luggage labels form the basis for gift tags? Think about your museum and what products, for which there would be a demand, could be made appropriate by being put in a relevant context. For example, sausages from the pork butcher's shop at the Blists Hill Site at Ironbridge Gorge Museum! Could you sell regional items (like Nottingham lace) or seasonal items. (In America a best selling item at the Mystic Seaport Museum is a Christmas Memory book in which you record details of your Christmases over 20 years. The Christmas Memory Book sold nearly 40,000 copies!)

You may want to develop items to give a bigger range of products, or fill gaps in your product range (for example, a suitable souvenir item for teenagers, or foreign visitors). If you have had successful items that have sold well you may try to strengthen your market by producing more, similar, items, thus providing existing customers with new, but similar, items (much in the way the National Trust has done so successfully in the last few years.) This strategy is particularly good at attracting regular shoppers to your museum shop, which they begin to rely on as a source of a particular style of goods.

When developing your own product range, you have to be aware of the manufacturing processes involved in production of different types of goods. For example, you need to know that to make an object in plastic or metal (as opposed to stamping a name or picture on an existing object) you will need to have a die made, this involves complicated and expensive tool making, and you will need to spread the costs of origination over a large quantity to keep the unit price down. Tea towels, and printed fabrics, involve the preparation of colour screens – the number of screens depends on the number of colours you use, but generally will not exceed four. You will have to pay about £70 for each colour screen, this is a once-off cost, but it means that if the particular item does not sell well you would not re-order, so the screen costs would have to be spread over relatively few units, and this may make your tea towel too expensive, or you may have to cut your profit margins on this

this initial order. Before you get involved in commissioning designs, ask the potential manufacturer for information on likely economic quantities. Tell him what you can, without being too specific – tell him you are only working on an idea, and want to know if it would be practicable. He will point out to you likely problem areas, and ways to avoid expense (for example, by keeping to two colours, or using a size compatible with his machine sizes). Once you know the rough costings you can see whether the project is feasible or not.

If you have confidence in the product but do not think you can afford to produce it, consider arranging a deal with a manufacturer where, in return for your idea and right to produce the item, linked with your museum's name, you can have products, and royalties. (See the section on deals with commercial companies.)

One acid test of any 'own' product is would you buy the item from another supplier? Too often the answer must be no. It is very usual to hear from those in museum trading how disappointed they were with a product they initiated – 'it didn't come out as we hoped'. It is usually because people believe that the rather tatty art work or design will be transformed by the manufacturing process. This is not the case – things will probably be slightly worse than the artwork! Sometimes, it is the medium itself which cannot really replicate the original – for example, modern, inexpensive stained glass will not have the lustre and colour of the priceless original. Measured against the original item it was inspired by, your product may be disappointing, but how does it stand up as an item in its own right; does it represent value for money? Does it compare well with other similar items? Does it reflect your museum's image and standards of excellence? These are more realistic criteria than comparing it against the original.

Safety

Under the Consumer Protection Act (1961) and the Consumer Safety Act (1978) the manufacturer, wholesaler, importer or retailer can all be prosecuted for selling goods which do not adhere to certain specified standards. Orders are made under the Acts, as the need arises, to stop some particularly dangerous manufacturing technique or practice. There is a list of items covered (ranging from motor bikes to oil heaters). Most are not likely to be items stocked by a museum shop, though toys, aerosols, and glazed ceramic ware, which are all covered, may well be sold by museum shops. The Department of Trade will supply a list of regulations under the Acts on request.

If you buy from a reputable manufacturer you will usually assume that the safety is guaranteed. For things like toys, where safety is important, ask the manufacturer if the goods conform to the relevant British Standards Institution standards (if his assurance is too bland ask for the actual BSI number).

You cannot be certain that everything you sell is absolutely safe, but you should adopt the care of a reasonable person. If people use an item for purposes other than its intended use it is hardly your fault if it is dangerous. But be careful, especially with toys, to see that items are sufficiently well made that they do not come apart, revealing sharp edges – the most common cause of accidents. Do not sell goods that your are worried about – the potential damage to the museum's reputation is not worth the possible financial gain.

Specific items

Apart from general considerations of what to stock it may be useful to consider in detail certain specific items that can be considered as the back-bone of museum trading.

Postcards

The post-card is the item most generally stocked in a museum shop. Virtually every museum shop will offer postcards for sale, and the larger the shop the larger the selection. Because it is of low value, it is scarcely economic to handle, especially if bought singly, and it requires substantial investment, since to produce postcards economically one has to print relatively long runs. Yet every museum shop feels obliged to stock some postcards, because it will be argued it is an item the customer may expect, actually it is because those running museum shops expect to find postcards in museums. One could almost measure the commercial acumen of those running museum shops with the proportion and range of the stock held in postcards. (Art galleries would be allowed a higher proportion, because of the relevance of the postcards to their collection.) There is no doubt that a museum shop can sell a great many postcards. In some shops 70% of the turnover comes from sales of post-cards. But instead of believing this figure vindicates tying up a great deal of stock in postcards, it should really be used as a terrible lesson. If your shop is to maximise profits you should have a higher proportion of sales of higher value than a 15p postcard. You can, in fact, increase the value of post-card sales by selling them in theme packs – say 10 postcards of ceramics, or 10 of textile designs or by a single artist. The customer would probably prefer to make his individual selection, and buy cards singly – but can you afford the display space, the capital investment in a wide range of subjects, and the time involved in stock control of many different postcard designs. Perhaps we should learn the lesson set by the most commercial of any museum trading – the Metropolitan Museum in New York – there in the shops in the museum, amongst an enormous range of goods, a bigger selection than can be found in any UK museum, indeed, probably by a factor of five, there are probably no more than two hundred postcards, whereas in the major English museums one finds nearly a thousand different postcards are routinely stocked. At the Metropolitan in New York those in charge of trading will argue that they are trying to increase the value of individual sales, that if a visitor wants a reproduction or a picture they could buy it in a more expensive form, such as a print or a greetings card. The UK habit of offering a very substantial range of postcards should be seen as little more than a habit. One factor is that it is easier to produce postcards than to devise other goods.

Obviously the picture on the postcard is what will sell it. Either it shows some interesting item of a museum's collection, or a painting or drawing, or a view of a building or the scenery. Clearly the attractiveness of the picture matters. Take trouble at this stage to choose a visually attractive item, and make sure the transparency of it you supply to the printer is also attractive. One only has to glance at a selection of picture postcards in any holiday town to be aware of the very low standard of photography that can slip through. Check the

35

transparency for colour accuracy (the photographer must get his lighting right to get an accurate image). You have to decide if you are going to reproduce the whole, or part, of the picture, and whether to have a border, or let the image 'bleed' – that is, be taken right to the edge.

It will be cheaper to use a specialist postcard printer rather than a jobbing printer, since he will be equipped for the job. The specialist postcard printer usually asks for a minimum order of 3,000 cards of any one design. Some will ask for at least five or six designs to be ordered at any one time, but several of the biggest companies handle so many orders that they can fit in several orders together in one print run. The specialist printers can complete orders in as little as three or four weeks, but others may take longer. Ask about printing schedules when placing the original order, as it is important to know because of the need to re-order. Also you need to have your cards when you have visitors to buy them, not after the season is finished. The going rate for postcards in 1986 seems to be around £160 (+ VAT) for 3,000 of one design, falling as the quantity is increased to around £340 (+ VAT) for 10,000. If you order say 8 designs at a time you can expect a reduction of at least 20% overall. These are all inclusive prices – including a colour proof prior to printing. If you use a fine art printer, who is geared up to postcards, but working to a higher standard than the ordinary postcard printer then you will pay more.

Generally museums and galleries undercharge for their postcards. Remember to re-price old stock, so that all postcards of similar size and quality are the same. Price at a level which simplifies change giving – for example, 15p not 16p or 14p. You have to price post-cards at, to some extent, a level similar to your competitors, or at least on roughly the same scale, so that you do not arouse visitor suspicions! The appropriate price for London and the South East certainly seems to be 15p, whereas in the less affluent North of the country there is some sales resistance if cards are 15p – the customer expects them to be 10p! (It is worth museums with large numbers of foreign visitors noting that in museums in the USA, and in most of continental Europe, postcards are more expensive, generally the equivalent of 20–25p.)

When deciding how many different designs of postcards to stock, ask yourself at what level of range will I start losing sales? Will I sell more postcards by increasing the number of designs, or sell the same number, but give the customer more choice? By careful monitoring you can judge at what level of variety you should fix your postcard range. If your range is large, you are tying up a great deal of capital, in items which may be slow selling (drop the slowest selling postcards and just re-print the popular ones, and introduce new designs in small quantities to test them before placing a substantial order). Remember not all your visitors re-visit, so although you may want a change of designs because you are bored, they may not! If you have postcards that are really unsaleable – or are selling at the rate of 100 a year, so you have at least 28 years' supply, give them to school children who visit the museum – they will be very pleased, and it will clear the stock room!

Greetings cards

You can use the same images you use on postcards to produce greetings cards. These can be sold singly or in packs. There is a strong argument for selling in packs, say of 10, because the value of the item is increased (also it means you get rid of 10 times the quantity at a time). Greetings cards can be seasonal – for example, Christmas cards – or for every day use, with no greeting inside. Christmas cards are nearly always bought by the end user (the person using them) but everyday cards may also be bought as a gift item to give to someone else, so the packaging and presentation becomes more important in increasing sales. The British Museum is amongst the museums offering very attractive folders of greetings cards, with the design shown on the outside of the folder. If you are not ordering in sufficient quantities to cover the cost of the expensive packaging you may order heavy gauge plastic wallets, into which you can pack, as sales require, cards and envelopes of various designs.

Greetings cards sell on design. If the picture on the front is pretty the card will sell, if it is not, however interesting the object it illustrates, however seminal in the development of Western civilization, it will not sell. Of course, not everyone has the same view of what is a pretty picture. Use the sales of postcards as a guide. Always be prepared to learn from the customers. You may hate a picture, indeed nearly all museum curators despise certain Victorian genre pictures, of saccharine sweetness, which are very good subjects for

37

greetings cards! Your concern is not with the quality of the original painting.

If you have enough customers you can produce your own greetings cards. There are several schemes offering shared print runs for greetings cards — some from postcard printers (who offer a minimum of 3,000 cards with envelopes for £330 + VAT, at 1986 prices. The figure reduces quite substantially as the quantity increases.) Alternatively museums can join the print runs of the Charity Christmas Card Scheme, which offers printing on a non-profit basis, to charities and museums alike. The Scheme will print a design from the museum, with the museum having to buy only 2,500 providing a charity shares the design; or the museum can have an exclusive, with a larger commitment. In 1986, the cost would be, depending on size, including packing in 10s in cellobags and labelling, substantially less than £200 for 2,500 cards. Like all printing the unit cost falls as the quantity increases. The Charity Christmas Card Scheme, as its name suggests, specialises in Christmas cards, but it can also print everyday cards on the same board as its Christmas cards. It carries as stock items certain museum cards, which can be bought in small quantities, a minimum of ten packs of a design.

Other card manufacturers carry stocks of cards of museum subjects, which can be bought in small quantities. Make sure that any card manufacturer asking for reproduction rights on any of your pictures is asked, as a condition of reproduction, to supply cards at 'run on' cost (that is the marginal cost of printing). Ask other museums if they would like to exchange goods such as greetings cards with you — for example, have 50 packs of each other's designs. This increases the variety you can offer, without costing you anything.

The Christmas card market is enormous. Many museums are selling an increasing number of Christmas cards, and most find that although sales peak at the end of November and early December, they still have significant sales to the tourists in the summer if the cards are available then. It is not worth mounting a full-blown display before October, but it is worth having some cards available and on show. Some museums have built up a regular clientele for cards — they are known to stock a good range, and the locals will pay a special visit to the museum shop to buy their cards. Museum Christmas cards like charity cards give people the opportunity to show their goodwill — and proclaim it to their friends. You can help capitalise on this by having a sign above your cards, or marking each pack, indicating that the card is sold in aid of the museum's work. The Bodleian Library has been particularly successful over the past few years in building up its Christmas card sales. Once you have people coming to buy Christmas cards you can increase your range of other gift items, such as tags, wrapping paper and use the opportunity to increase sales overall, as people buy gift items.

Cheap souvenir items

There are manufacturers of 'souvenir' items, who will produce goods with your name and logo on, such as bookmarks, key fobs, pens, erasers, rulers, purses, comb cases, balloons, notepads (of all shapes and sizes), mugs, hats; the list is enormous and frequently changing. Where do you find such manufacturers? Generally, you do not have to worry, they will find you! They will offer you 'new lines', 'best sellers', 'wonderful notions'. All you have to do is exercise caution in the face of their enthusiasm. Limit the number of these low cost souvenir lines – because the main customers for them, children, will be quite content with a choice of say six items – any more simply slows down the time it takes to make a decision and if you are dealing with a coachload of children, and the teacher is getting hysterical because they are late, you want to simplify the process. Also, it is better, since the turnover of these items in a busy museum shop is very fast, to keep significant quantities of each item both on display and as back-up stock, and it is easier to do this with a small range of goods, rather than a large one, because of the handling, the storage space and the amount of display space. Also you want to limit your investment, and this is best done by limiting the number of 'lines'.

Be cautious in your ordering – test all new items with a small initial order, and only re-order the best sellers. (Out of 6 souvenir 'lines' you may be testing one or two new lines at a time.) Take care to have the stocks when you need them. Find out about delivery dates and 'lead times' (that is, the time needed to get a delivery from the time of the order). If an item takes seven days from time of order to delivery then you can afford to order in relatively small quantities and re-order as and when necessary. If an item takes six weeks, and this is a more usual time for goods which have to be stamped with your logo, then you must plan carefully so that you have sufficient stocks to coincide with what may be your short season. You do not want to miss sales, nor do you want to have to pay for stock which will sit in your store-room from October to May.

Apart from limiting the number of cheap souvenir items on practical grounds you should also limit them because they will impose their style on your shop. Your more expensive goods will suffer by association with cheap souvenirs. The first impression of your shop could lead a potential customer to dismiss it as not for them because they think your stock is all at the same level as the cheap souvenir items. These items are not so dreadful, or you would not stock them at all, but they do proclaim their nature – which is an inexpensive, novelty item, aimed at children and teenagers – and whilst not exactly tasteless they are not in good taste. They should be displayed in bulk, helping to reinforce the impression of them as cheap, cheerful items, and their impact confined to a particular part of the shop.

Not all souvenir items have to fall into the tacky category, but there are very few generally available souvenirs that fall outside this category (witness the Design Centre's occasional desperate attempts to find good souvenirs!). Museums have often produced very nice souvenir items specifically for their own museums. For example, Ironbridge Gorge Museum Trust has a cast iron bottle opener, marked 'The Iron Bridge, erected 1779', the Bethnal Green Museum has lead soldiers, originally offered on sale at £1 each but now a more daunting £3. The Victoria and Albert Museum has a range of excellent notebooks, and the Royal Academy can offer everything from own label bottles of wine to PVC aprons.

Books

Like postcards, virtually every museum shop will stock books, to a greater or lesser extent. There is rarely any question that a book is an appropriate item for the shop to sell. There can, of course, be a dispute over which publications should be stocked, with the argument dividing on popular versus scholarly lines. Ideally, the museum may be an important focus for education in its community.

The shop may reflect this by offering a good range of books on local history and the geography of the region. In some areas the museum shop may provide the town's leading serious bookshop on such subjects, but also on art. (In some American communities the museum shop is the most important source of serious children's books in the town.)

The museum shop should offer a range of books, in subject and style. For example, the museum may have a large ceramic collection. It will want to offer popular books about how to make china and pottery, books with plenty of illustrations, to attract the general reader, and more detailed, scholarly works say about 18th century decoration on china. The museum may also be an important tourist attraction in the area, and so as a service to its visitors it will want to offer books about the surrounding countryside, and towns, and their attractions. There may, indeed, be a very good demand for books about the region, such as Regional Cookery books, or books of photographs of the area at the turn of the century. If the area is known for a particular craft, which presumably will be represented in the museum's collection (though there may be another specialist museum in the town) then books on the subject may also be considered relevant.

Most of your visitors will have a general, not informed interest in your collection, and so you must cater for them when offering books. Clearly, to capture their interest you will want to offer books with illustrations, with attractive covers, with titles which clearly indicate content; to attract the general reader the packaging of the book becomes important. Have a range of books to cover all age ranges (children to grannies) and various interest and educational levels. Stock books to coincide with any publicity for them (for example, to coincide with television serials or series) and try not to be the last one to know – for example, when the eighth customer has asked for a particular book and you remark they are the eighth person to ask (and find you had not got the book) and you are told 'Oh, it must be because it is the Book at Bedtime serial', you have missed your sales. (The publishers' 'reps' will keep you abreast of any promotions.)

You will want to stock some scholarly books, out of a sense of duty, because although they are slow selling items, stocking them lends credibility to your shop's educational role, helps support scholarship, and helps maintain or establish your shop's reputation as a specialist bookshop. You may have your own publications such as catalogues and monographs and these may be the slowest selling items of all!

Anyone selling books is bound by the NET Book Agreement to sell that book for the publisher's recommended retail price. (Some books are non NET, but very few, and if you are publishing a book you can fix the price as you wish.) The profit margin on books is usually 35%, so they are a less profitable item than gift items, which normally have a profit margin of 50%. (For example, disregarding VAT on the gift item — £100 invested in stock of books can earn you, gross, £50, since its retail value is £150, but £100 invested in gifts can earn you £100 since its retail value is £200). It helps if you are handling relatively expensive books, so the actual profit is higher, though the percentage mark-up is the same. But most books in the museum shop are 'impulse buys' and there are few people who can afford to buy £50 art books, on an impulse. The average value of books sold in the museum shops which have significant sales of books is £5–£10. With the more expensive books there is an additional problem of damage during handling — which means the book is unsaleable except at a high discount. If you keep expensive books wrapped in cellophane, or behind glass, you sell fewer, so you are in a quandary. Ideally, you sell enough to have one inspection copy for customers to handle, and keep all the others wrapped. (Ask the publishers to supply the inspection copy free.)

To get any discount from a publisher you usually just have to send an official order, and make clear the books are for re-sale. Some publishers may insist that they give discounts only to members of the Booksellers Association. You can apply for membership, but your application could be opposed by a local bookshop, so it may be diplomatic to discuss the proposal beforehand with any local booksellers. You should make it clear to them that you would be a specialist bookseller, and not a general bookshop, and that you would not, like them, be attempting to subsidise sales of serious books by selling pulp fiction, thus taking away their main trade. If you are buying substantial quantities of any one book then ask the publisher for a quantity discount (this may be up to an additional 10%). The publisher will never volunteer a discount — you have to ask for it!

The best way to know what books to stock is to look at other museum shops and bookshops, read The Bookseller, which generally has information on all new titles, and build up a relationship with the publishers' 'reps' (their travelling salesmen). The 'reps' will come and show you new titles they think you might want, and will tell you of any promotions of the publication that are planned. It is the publisher's 'rep' who can be asked to arrange visits by the author for autographing sessions, or for special sales cards and posters. Keep in touch with small publishers who may not have 'reps' and ask them to keep you abreast of relevant publications. Tell other museums you are interested in stocking their publications, perhaps on a reciprocal basis.

If you order books that do not sell, most of the major publishers will allow you to return unsold copies (over-stocks) and will credit your account accordingly. This is a system that must not be abused – or the facility will be withdrawn. You should not return too soon after publication (they will feel you have not given the book a fair chance) or too late after publication (when the publisher will have difficulty in re-selling the book elsewhere). It is best to ask in advance if the publisher will extend these 'see safe' terms to you.

Display of books is important, especially in attracting the general, non-specialist, who is making an impulse buy. Where space permits, books should be displayed 'face out' – the front cover on display, not just the spine, as in an ordinary bookshelf. It helps to have a 'new books' table, on which books, or catalogues, can be piled up. This helps create interest, adds impact, and should encourage the casual shopper with limited time to glance at the books, when a more concentrated assault on close packed bookshelves is too daunting. Scholarly books, with little general appeal can be kept on conventional book-shelves – because the more committed visitor will take the trouble to search them out. Make sure that you follow the same principle with books as all merchandise, give the best selling position to the best selling items. Make sure you do not run out of fast-selling books – keep more than one copy out in the shop if you expect to sell several copies each day, because it is impractical to keep having to run to the stock room, and there is also a good chance you will not notice that you have no copies on display until you have an enquiry (and you have probably lost sales by then). Keep the books well dusted, particularly slow selling books need to be taken off the shelves, and shelf and book dusted. If you do not, dust will lie on these rarely disturbed items, which adds to their unsaleability.

Consider the atmosphere which most people expect when they go into a bookshop. It is quiet, there is a serious atmosphere, and the quiet browser must feel at ease. If you are hoping to sell books in any substantial quantity, then you will have to ensure that there is at least a part of your shop which has the atmosphere of a bookshop. (In essence this means physically separating books from the school parties.)

Replicas

A replica is an exact copy of an item in your collection. Whilst the replica may be of a different size, for example, a six foot high statue may be reproduced one foot high, the scale should be maintained and the overall appearance be such that it be recognised as a copy of the original. Copying original works has a long history, indeed in the past centuries without photography or television, however else did people see the artistic wonders of the world, except by being shown copies? The Ruskin Gallery at Sheffield provides an interesting example of a museum in significant part devoted to the display of Victorian copies of antique works.

Although records show the British Museum was producing replicas as early as 1817, it is only since the 1960's that the production of replicas has mushroomed, so that for some museums, such as the British Museum, sales of replicas account for a high proportion of sales, through the shop, by mail order and sales to the trade. The increase in the production of replicas has been a concomitant of the rise of museum trading, but it is also due to the emergence of materials and techniques which have made it possible to produce cheap copies of reasonable quality. For example, the Percy Panels from the Castle Museum in York which are of carved wood, are replicated in resin with a high degree of visual authenticity.

Virtually any item in your collection can be copied. The main problem is to produce copies of sufficient quality cheaply enough. The medium is usually the main determinant of whether an item can be copied successfully. Where one is substituting a cheaper material for the original, for example silver gilt for gold, there will be a loss of the intrinsic beauty of the original material, but it may be possible (through moulding) to replicate the craftsmanship at least.

44

Similarly, an ivory netsuke reproduced in resin loses much of its original beauty which was in the intrinsic beauty of the ivory, but it is a fair representation of the original at a fraction of the cost. In fact the craftsmanship involved in making replicas, for example, in moulding, hand colouring and finishing, is nowhere as great as that of the original craftsmen. In part, this is simply because today's labour costs reduce the time that can be spent on making the item. In other cases, for example, in printing, since machines do the work, the skills built over years of practice have disappeared. In other cases processes have been lost – for example, we can no longer produce the true cobalt colouring of a Staffordshire figure. When planning a reproduction you must be aware of what is feasible at the cost you are prepared to incur. Listen to the manufacturers, and be guided by their expertise. (Of course, make sure you are dealing with a manufacturer who is capable of good quality work). There are developments all the time which are extending the range of possible reproduction.

When selecting an item for reproduction make sure you have copyright (this will only arise on items of relatively recent manufacture – almost everything pre 1870 will be out of copyright). If you do not own copyright it is often relatively easy to get the consent of the copyright owner – since helping the museum is seen as a good thing! Make sure you copyright your replicas! It is ethically correct to mark all replicas as such, with your museum imprint on the actual item, because otherwise unscrupulous antique dealers have been known to do a brisk trade in selling copies as originals. Replicas of coins are often produced without the reverse side design, which avoids any possible confusion.

How do you decide what to reproduce? The first criteria must be the attractiveness of the item. Something that is very pretty will at least stand a chance of being pretty in reproduction. Something that is rather dull is unlikely to be transformed by being copied. Remember that if anything you lose in reproduction (usually because the material is less attractive or the craftsmanship inferior, or the patina of age missing). An item of mass manufacture, for example, Victorian advertising material will be easier to replicate satisfactorily than an item whose attraction was in the craftsmanship and beauty of its material, because you cannot replicate these. Replicas do not always have to be wonderful reproductions, capturing the essence of the original to sell. The Lewis chessmen produced

by the British Museum sell well because the original design is so
spirited and whilst much is lost in reproduction, the item is still overwhelmingly appealing.

Reproductions range from copies of old cards or other printed
material right through to casts of sculpture, or copies of china or
jewellery. There are more replicas of jewellery and small metal
items, such as seals, spoons and coins, than of any other categories
of items (though greetings cards must be coming a close second).
Perhaps, people think that small items are more saleable, or perhaps
it is simply easier to have certain items reproduced because there is a
known designer and manufacturer to do it, so making the process
much easier.

Replicas of printed items can provide a very inexpensive and attractive souvenir. The British Library's copies of Magna Carta; the
Monmouth Museum's reproduction of the rules for school attendance and the Cambridge and County Folk Museum's replicas of
Victorian homiles, are bargain priced souvenirs. Whilst the
products of the Monmouth and Cambridge Museums were not reproduced to the standard of the originals, as items for less than 20p
they certainly offered school children a change from the usual.
Some museums are in fact holding original printing blocks and
etching plates and there are instances of these being used to produce
replicas (or should one say, extend the original print runs?) Tyne
and Wear Museums Services have produced an attractive range of
five prints of 19th Century views of Tyneside from original plates
(coated first to protect against additional wear). This is a very imaginative use of the museum's collection, which has been deservedly
successful. It is interesting to note that the printing is on rag paper,
to reproduce the quality of the originals.

When choosing an object to replicate you must take especial care to
see it is not damaged by excessive handling, or from having a mould
taken from it. Curatorial staff are rightly jealous of objects in their
custody, and there have been several reprehensible cases of damage
being caused in the process of copies being made. Make sure the
manufacturer comes with references. Check up to see that the item is
always treated appropriately. Once an item has been damaged you
are unlikely ever to have access to another one, so your planned
programme of replica production will come to an abrupt end!

Pricing replicas can be very difficult. You have to consider the cost
of manufacture and the cost of similar items (for example, a gold ring

should be within the usual range of gold ring prices). What is the likely market for the product, and what do customers expect to pay for similar items. (This is perhaps the most crucial consideration.) It may be sensible to have some highly priced replicas in your shop to add tone to the whole place. It does have to be apparent to the customer why the item is expensive – is it the material, is it the obvious craftsmanship, is it the size? (If one looks at the range of replicas on offer from the Musee du Louvre it is easy to understand that a 5 foot high replica is going to cost a great deal). We have expectations in our mind of what things should cost (the technical phrase is 'the perceived value'). In producing replicas it is important to price the items in line with people's expectations.

Replicas have the advantage of being clearly relevant to a museum's collection. They are generally produced on quite a small scale, involving quite short production runs, although the initial cost of tooling is often quite considerable. Replicas should be seen as a long-lasting item of stock – giving one the opportunity to recover the origination costs. It is quite usual to either write off the origination costs, or to reckon to recover them quickly, and see every replica after, say, the first 100, as being highly profitable, whereas the first 100 carried all the development cost. How you work out a formula is really up to you, and your finance officer.

Summary

Choose stock that will reflect creditably on the museum set criteria for selecting stock. Make sure you have enough stock to be able to generate sales at a level to cover your overheads. Work out target stock-turn. Plan your stock, with reference to your budget. You can find goods by seeing what other museums stock, by visiting trade fairs and through manufacturers' approaches. You can develop your own products if you have funds to invest.

Producing items inspired by the museum's collection.
Trevor Jones, *formerly Head of Publications, Birmingham Museum and Art Gallery.*

That the museums and art galleries of this country are adopting – in terms of publishing – an aggressive, entrepreneurial attitude towards the commercial exploitation of their collections is now no longer newsworthy. Whilst there are still institutions where initiatives are stifled by the weight of bureaucracy, there are many more where the considerable advantages of a lively publishing programme are well recognised. The extent to which this recognition translates into an effective and profitable activity does, of course, vary considerably between different organisations (and is not, significantly, related merely to size or visitor headcount).

It does, however, seem possible to identify those factors which, in a variety of permutations, are likely to enhance the possibility of success in this area of work:

1. *A recognition by senior management that it is insufficient for policies to be adopted, and targets identified, without ensuring that those responsible for implementing the programme will receive a reasonable level of co-operation from their colleagues. This is perhaps largely a matter of education and can even be simply a matter of crude coercion: co-operation in supplying transparencies for a commercial calendar will produce funds for the production of a scholarly catalogue. This point is fundamental: there are many frustrated Publications Officers who are attempting to discharge their duties with their hands tied.*

2. *It follows from this that members of the curatorial staff are more likely to be positive in their attitude towards a publications programme if they can be confident that material curated by them will be used by their publishing colleagues in an appropriate fashion. What is appropriate is, of course, sometimes a contentious point (and certainly varies from one organisation to another, let alone amongst individuals within the same institution) but it is unlikely that no common ground exists between curatorial and publishing staff in this context. Some concessions on both sides are likely to be necessary.*

3. *The museum publisher should be able to lay valid claim to the excellence of the quality of his product. Unhappily, there is too*

much still produced by (often, major) museums and galleries which is mediocre and meritritious. The fact that rubbish will sell should be wholly irrelevant: quality of concept, of design and of production should be paramount. It very often is not, and perhaps provides an example of a wholly inappropriate financial pressure being exerted.

4. *An awareness of what is being produced and sold in the world outside museums and galleries is of huge importance. Since fashion plays a large part in this, research in this area needs to be continual. It can be as informal as simply noting what new products appear in the shops and as strenuous as a regular attendance at the major Trade Fairs (in the U.K., for example, the N.E.C. Spring Fair and the Gift Fair at Harrogate).*

Concomitant with this is a willingness to plagiarise any idea which has potential as a museum/gallery product. Consider, for example, the number of art-based diaries and address books which the market has been capable of absorbing in recent years!

5. *An enthusiasm for the principle of co-operation between institutions (and, by implication, a knowledge of what projects are in prospect elsewhere). The advantages of co-operation, in terms of larger quantities and of lower unit costs, are obvious; knowing what others are planning will avoid the prospect, at the moment probably inevitable, of two museums or galleries separately but simultaneously producing what are effectively identical products. There is perhaps an argument for the establishment of a 'clearing house' where major publishing initiatives could be registered, in order to both pre-empt duplication and to encourage joint participation.*

6. *The museum or gallery which establishes a close working relationship with an appropriate commercial distributor or distributors is likely to benefit greatly as a result: as indeed, hopefully, will the distributor. Projects which lack viability when sold solely from the Museum shop assume very different proportions when distribution to the trade is in prospect. Profit per unit on trade sales is likely to be modest, but the volume and the effect of increased production quantities on the overall unit cost can be significant. Contact with the sharp end of Commerce can be salutary: if the distributor isn't enthusiastic, should the*

project be abandoned? And can the museum or gallery, as publisher, work to the timetable imposed by a commercial liaison? The committee system and commerce are often not happy bedfellows.

These various factors, of course, merely underpin two basic assumptions – that an institution's Collections are capable of sustaining a lively and innovative publishing activity, and that a competent decision-making structure exists in order that the material may be exploited. The final element is perhaps the most crucial – an awareness that publishing is a speculative activity, and that an expectation of a constant stream of successes is hardly realistic. Decisions need to be made on the basis of a broad overview of a programme rather than – as tends to be the case where public funds are involved – as a result of over-reaction to a specific achievement or failure. Less successful ventures will, hopefully, be absorbed by the runaway best-sellers; but museum and gallery publishing, like every other form of publishing, will always carry an element of risk. Prudent planning, market research and pre-selling can do no more than reduce this factor; it is rarely possible to eliminate it wholly.

Deals with Commercial Companies

An increasing number of companies are offering museums co-publishing or royalty deals, if the museum allows the company to produce items either based on, or straight reproductions of items in the museum's collections. As well as providing the design source the museum is, in effect, lending its name to the product, sometimes as a quite specific endorsement. Whilst you are not exactly supping with the devil when dealing with commercial companies, you certainly have to be aware that the more successful the company the harder the bargain they will try to strike. The commercial company owe loyalty to their company, their shareholders, their owners, whoever, not to the museum. However much they protest to have the museum's best interest at heart, you must be aware this is not the case. Why should it be? It is much better if both sides are quite clear as to their motives; what they want from the deal, and what constraints they have (these are likely to be more on the museum's side).

There are different types of commercial deals that the museum may be offered.

Co-publishing

Co-publishing, where the commercial publisher produces a publication together with the museum, is very helpful to museums as a way of producing publications with reduced capital outlay. The deal that you can strike depends largely on the marketability of the end product. For example, a commercial publisher may undertake to produce a series of fully-illustrated books, the text prepared, and thus approved, by the museum's curatorial staff and the design of the publication approved by the museum. The museum may have to provide no capital beyond a commitment to sell the publication at the museum. The publisher knows that the museum will have steady sales of the publication, so knows the investment is not very risky.

There are companies which specialise in producing guide books for museums and stately homes, who have no market for the product beyond the museum itself, yet because they are sure of the market they are prepared to fund the whole publication. The museum (or stately home) has a great deal of control over the publication – usually supplying the text. The design follows a tried and tested format. Why does the company undertake the publication of the guide book – because it calculates that the museum will sell sufficient copies for it to make a profit. The company is sufficiently experienced to know whether a particular site is likely to generate sufficient sales to warrant its investment (they are likely to be uninterested if you have fewer than 100,000 visitors a year, because the economics of guide book production, with full colour printing throughout, means that the print runs have to be long to keep the unit price sufficiently low to sell at the appropriately low price). These guide books are supplied to the museum at the standard 35% publisher's discount. It is clear to both sides what the arrangement is, and since the publication follows a standard pattern, the museum is unlikely to be surprised by what it gets. The only grounds for disappointment are usually the quality of the colour reproductions (and to be fair these are usually of quite good standard). The publisher, on the other hand, may be disappointed by the level of sales the museum achieves – but that is what commercial risk is all about – so do not feel upset or guilty!

When producing books the publisher may ask for the museum to make a commitment to take say a thousand or two thousand copies on publication, and this means the museum is in effect having to fund part of the costs of publication. The terms the publisher will impose will depend on how well he thinks he will be able to sell the publication to outlets other than the museum. If you have a very good collection full of attractive items, and your museum is prestigious, then the publisher will be more sympathetic, and more anxious to offer terms attractive enough to tempt you into a co-publishing deal than if you are a small, relatively unknown museum, with a not particulary visually attractive collection. The publisher wants the museum's sales to pay for the production costs, and other sales provide his profits. The diaries and address books produced by, for example, Alan Hutchison Publishing for the Victoria & Albert Museum, or Hunkydory for Birmingham Museum, or Abydos for the National Trust, are all examples of co-publishing. The deals have varied enormously; in some cases the museum has had to pay for as few as 400 copies on publication, in other cases the museum has had to commit itself to 2,500 copies. The costs have varied from cost price + 10p to the standard publishers discount of 35%. 40% seems a more usual arrangement.

As well as the better discount it may be offered on the publications it sells through its shop, the museum may also be offered a royalty on sales to other outlets (most usually 10%, but again this may vary and can be as low as 2½%). Sometimes the museum may be offered an initial fee which may or may not be treated like an author's advance, as a pre-payment of royalties. It all depends on how much the commercial company thinks it will benefit by publishing a particular item. This may be calculated simply on anticipated profits, or it may have a more indirect benefit of bringing prestige and credibility to the publisher. The publisher's motives are usually quite clear in co-publishing deals, and it is quite in order for the museum to ask to have them spelt out – for example, asking at the outset how many copies are to be published, how many sold to outlets other than the museum, how will they be sold, how will the museum's involvement be shown, and whether the publisher expects to market the book in conjunction with others, and if so which? A co-publication is very innocuous when sold in a museum shop. Is it quite so neutral if it is seen in company with other titles with which the museum would not want to be associated. Put at its crudest would you want a publication on 18th century life to be sold alongside sensational publications on 'Famous 18th Century Whores' and 'Flagellation in the 18th Century'? The time to ask the questions is before, not after! It is surprising how many co-publishing deals leave the museums feeling cheated. Often they are quite unrealistic. They give the publishers too little credit for their ability to sell to a wider market. In most cases the museums themselves could not sell as effectively as the commercial publishers (they are not geared up to do so). But it is not impossible for them – and thus for example the Tate Gallery has successfully produced its own diary – and the important thing is that the museum learns from the co-publishing experience, so that it can judge whether or not next time it should co-publish or try to earn for itself the publisher's profits by publishing and marketing for itself.

Licensing

There is no question but that licensing is the great growth area in museum trading. The levels of money to be earned from licensing deals makes one wonder why one bothers with any other form of trading! Licensing means that you allow a manufacturer to use material in your collection as the basis for his products. Usually, but not inevitably, your museum is identified with the product, and this association is exploited to help sell the merchandise.

You have to have the stomach for licensing. Both the people you will deal with and their style of promoting the goods will probably seem very brash to any staff working in the museum. (One publications officer of a national museum said of a licensing agent, the middleman who arranged a licensing deal, 'Count your fingers after you shake hands with him!'). The licensing business is full of fast-talking persuaders. If the deal comes off then the rewards (for the marketeer) are high, so a great deal of hard-selling takes place. The museum is right to remain cautious, and must not be dazzled by all the oversize promises of pots of gold to agree to anything it might regret.

How do you go about setting up a licensing deal. Firstly, realise that the potential UK market is slight compared to the USA, where the idea of licensing is more established. The American market is not only larger, but it is also more used to co-ordinated ranges of goods, produced almost as fashion items. Also in the USA, the endorsement of good taste that association with a museum brings makes goods more marketable. So when being propositioned by a licensing broker it is worth paying particular attention to his experience of arranging deals with American manufacturers.

There are licensing brokers − that is their job, making licensing deals is their sole purpose. You may be approached by them, with the suggestion of a deal − or you approach them. There may be a particular item, or group of items in your collection which is ripe for exploitation, of which either you or the licensing agent may be aware. Or it may be that your collection is so extensive, and your name so prestigious – like the Victoria & Albert Museum – that the licensing agent will undertake to discover in your archives something suitable. The prime market for 'inspired by' items is the wallpaper, home furnishings market, together with co-ordinated stationery items. The licensing agent will arrange with the museum suggested ways in which the original product's design can be used. (The museum must always retain the right of veto.) There will, inevitably, be an adaptation of the original product – and in some cases the newly created range of goods owes very little to the original item – the term 'inspired by' may then be applied (and the museum can then be sure that it is selling its name as a promotional tool rather than its design!). The licensing agent will find the item on which the licensing deal is to be made, devise ways in which it can be adapted for modern manufacturers, and then approach either a manufacturer, for example a wallpaper manufacturer, or a retailer, who may want a co-ordinated range of goods, say as a 'spring' promotion. The licensing agent acts as the broker, and arranges the commercial deal.

What does the licensing agent charge, and what can the museum expect to get out of the deal financially? The licensing agent usually, but not always, may ask the museum for an initial fee. Alternatively, the museum may, if its product is sufficiently attractive, be offered an initial fee, which may, like an author's advance, be treated as a pre-payment, or may exceptionally be a straightforward payment. Both the museum and the licensing agent are paid on a royalty basis – the financial reward linked to the manufacturer's success. The level of royalties varies – the museum's share can be around 6% or can drop to 2%. The licensing agent can expect a royalty of 2% dropping to 1% as sales reach a certain level. The scale of the likely manufacturer's revenue from the deal can reach $10M, so if the museum has a 2% share it can earn as much as £200,000. There is nothing sacrosanct about any of these figures – it is up to the museum to strike the best deal it can (and be aware that the licensing agent and the manufactuer will all be looking after their own interests, and it may be at the museum's expense).

It is really very difficult for museum staff to feel that they are successful negotiators when in the company of licensing agents, because the style is different. It is unlikely that a very brash, aggressive, 'up-front' businessman would feel at home working in a museum, even in its trading company. In fact, some museum people are very competent negotiators, and strike a very hard bargain, but because they do not feel as aggressive as those they are dealing with, and have a more gentlemanly approach they may have tremendous self-doubts about their bargaining ability. It is very difficult for them to feel that they could possibly have been successful faced with such dynamic thrust! To strike a good bargain you must be clear what your parameters are, and make them clear to all concerned. To calculate what is a fair price, you have to decide what profits are likely to derive from the project. Ask the manufacturer what he proposes to make, get a rough idea of how much it will cost him, and what he will sell it for. (If he will not give full information you can probably get a good idea by comparing similar products, and getting a wholesale price list). Judge how much he expects to make on the deal. Ask him – it seems impertinent, but you really need that information.

You cannot commit the museum publicly to a deal that you do not have full information about. Too many cases of 'deals' in which the museum, or charity, is seen as the gullible victim of sharp commercial practice appear as exposés in the newspapers, for any deal to be lightly entered into.

You do not need to use a licensing agent to fix up licensing deals. The Royal Pavilion at Brighton arranged a licensing deal with an American wallpaper manufacturer without an agent – the then Director of the Pavilion on a visit to America simply contacted the manufacturer and made the deal, and earned for the Pavilion royalties now in excess of £140,000! A major national museum used a licensing agent who arranged a £150,000 deal for the museum. (It illustrates the difficulties of licensing deals that despite the large sum of money involved, the management of the museum were unhappy enough about the agreement that the money was paid into a frozen account.)

Licensing arrangements are not just to enable manufacturers to produce goods based on the museum's collection. That would simply be a matter of reproduction rights. It is quite clear that in licensing deals the manufacturer is using the association with the museum to help market his goods. The experience of the Museum of The City of New York in arranging licensing rights on reproductions of a picture of the Statue of Liberty which is in its collection, makes quite clear that it is the fact that the picture is reproduced with the consent of the museum that makes companies prepared to pay a licensing fee, rather than a reproduction fee. Of course, it is the astuteness of the Museum of the City of New York that this wish has been exploited to the extent of $½ million.

Copyright and reproduction rights

Normally the items in a museum's collection are out of copyright, because of their antiquity. But if someone wants to reproduce the item, most usually pictorially, they need a transparency or photograph, from which to copy. The museum may allow access, without charge, to any photographer, or it may, more usually, supply transparencies. The arrangements for supplying transparencies vary considerably. Museums may hire transparencies, or sell them. The charge is made usually according to a sliding scale, depending on the use. For example, if the picture is to be used as an illustration in a book it will be charged less than if it is to be a chocolate box cover. Charges are traditionally high for advertisers and low for publishers. Generally museums undercharge for reproduction rights.

The problems over reproduction rights are that it is very difficult to control. It is rare for the museum to have sole access to a picture of the item concerned (for example, there may be photographs from before the item was acquired and the major auction houses sell reproduction rights on items they sell) so it is hard to prove breach of copyright if a picture of the item is reproduced without consent. When hiring out transparencies it is difficult to prevent copies being made (even though you label the transparency with a stricture not to copy). The transparency is quite likely to be damaged in use (printers are notoriously careless) and the colours of any transparency exposed to strong light are going to fade. You may simply supply deteriorating transparencies, on the basis that it is the hirer's bad luck that his predecessors were careless, or you may try to keep a check on the transparencies, and charge highly so as to replace them frequently. Or you may decide that the job of administering a hire system is not worth the effort, and sell the transparencies.

Whichever method you use, try to keep track of the use of the transparency. It is usual to limit reproduction right to once only use.

This is hard to control. Mark your transparency, very inconspicuously, say with a dot, or slight scratch, so that you can identify, in reproduction, whether it derives from your copy. Make clear to users that if they want to use the transparency for more than one year they will have to pay a repeat fee. If the item is reproduced as part of a production run that will continue over several years, then fix a reproduction fee that takes this into account.

It is possible, apart from a straight reproduction fee combined with a hire or purchase fee on the transparency, to ask for a royalty from any manufacturer. Royalty deals need a certain amount of administration, but after all publishers manage, so it cannot be impossibly difficult. 6% is a very usual level of royalty to charge, but there is a great deal of room for negotiation, and the manufacturer's willingness to pay will depend on his estimate of how much he needs the reproduction rights.

What do you do if you discover that copies are being made of items in your collection, from your transparencies or prints, without your consent. This would be in breach of copyright, and you would be able to take legal action, and sue for compensation. It is sensible to work out a policy beforehand – not in very great detail, but just enough not to be taken unawares. Are you really going to sue? It is unlikely that you will want to get involved with lawyers, and the expense, unless the breach is flagrant, and stakes high. Usually a threat of suing should be enough to produce compensation. Devise with a lawyer a procedure which can start with the letter expressing pain 'We regret to learn that . . .' through to 'We shall be forced to take legal action' and culminating in the solicitor's letter (actually the culmination may indeed be the legal action itself). Try to fix a level of compensation for breach of copyright, again with a lawyer. It may be that you can work to a scale – inadvertent breach in a scholarly publication – warning and request for fees due; flagrant disregard of one year rule by a card manufacturer – fees due plus £25 punishment fee; flagrant disregard by a company standing to benefit greatly by use of the image – fees due plus compensation based on share of profits. You have to devise a system of penalties that you are likely to be able to enforce. It is not good fixing penalties which are so high that the offender elects to be sued and suffer the penalties imposed by the court

It is probably not worth getting paranoid about breaches of copyright. Certainly, it is very prevalent, and museums do suffer a loss of reproduction fees – but more is lost by fixing those fees too low in the first place.

You, or your trustees, may want to limit the use that can be made of reproductions. A usual restriction is not to allow a painting to be used as a jigsaw puzzle, as it is regarded as demeaning the image. Others would not like to see their pictures used on playing cards, sweatshirts, T-shirts, mugs, or in advertisements. As a museum or gallery you owe a debt to the artists, and may feel it is a breach of trust to allow the debasement of their work. All museums would argue that they would only allow reproductions that were in good taste. The interpretation of 'good taste' varies, so too does the individual museum's policies on reproductions. It is a policy matter that really should be taken with the agreement of the museum's director. Whilst it can be argued that by allowing a reproduction the museum is simply hiring out a transparency, it is extraordinary how in the public's mind the item produced may seem to have the museum's approval. (This is very like the apparent endorsements of goods through licensing deals, but without such justification.) Manufacturers may try to exploit this connection. It is interesting that a company criticised for producing what it claimed to be limited editions of a print of a painting in Glasgow Art Gallery (the criticism was that the print run of 1,000 copies was too great for it to be claimed as a limited edition) told the press that its prints were produced with the full consent of the artist 'and the copyright holder, Glasgow Art Gallery'. This brings the Gallery into an area of dispute that it cannot welcome.

Many museums and galleries are only too willing to allow manufacturers to reproduce items in the collection because they can thus have relevant goods to sell in their shop. Sometimes the museum will waive the reproduction fee in return for a supply of greetings cards or other items for re-sale. The museum should be sure of what it should ask for, and make sure it asks for enough. It may be better to ask to buy cards at 'run-on' cost. The manufacturer will be hoping to sell cards through the museum shop anyway, so do not be too grateful for an offer of discounted cards, remember you are selling his stock.

In all the types of deals you may strike with commercial companies be careful not to put the short-term gain before the long-term needs of the museum. The museum's reputation, its integrity as a repository of learning and culture, are more important than the short-term

59

and relatively insignificant financial benefit it may receive from deals with companies. Make sure that the deal is good for the museum not only in commercial terms. The sale of reproduction rights and licensing arrangements may popularise terms in the collection, and thus stimulate public interest in the museum, and encourage visitors. This is all to the good. But commerical exploitation of the museum's collection may also demean. It may bring the museum into disrepute not only amongst other museums, but amongst the educated public at large. The museum must, above all, preserve its good name. This does not mean it can avoid all efforts at money earning in the smug belief that it remains pure, unlike its sinful brethren. There is a middle way, which commonsense dictates. Museums should exploit their collections more, but take care to do so in a seemly, and dignified, manner.

Summary

Many companies now offer museums co-publishing or royalty deals. There is probably more money to be made from licensing and royalty deals than from any other aspect of trading, but museums should take care not to put short-term gain before the long term interests of the museum. There are great risks to the museum's good name.

Publicity

Opening a shop at the museum, with efficient signposting, cannot do more than attract those visiting the museum. You may want to attract to your shop customers who are not visiting the museum. This presupposes you are offering more than a few token souvenirs such as book marks, postcards and a guide book. If you are inviting people to visit your shop as an experience in its own right make sure you have enough stock to justify the visit. You may feel jubilant if you get people to come to the shop as as result of a series of 'small ads' in the local paper, but yours is a hollow victory if all they feel is disappointment.

If your shop can stand in its own right, with sufficient stock to make a visitor to it feel a special journey to the shop justified, then it is sensible to try to let other people know of its existence. Think who would find your shop most attractive, and then think of ways of contacting them. Decide on your most important attractions – perhaps you have the most comprehensive selection of art books for sale in the area; perhaps you offer a source of unusual gifts, perhaps your shop is the best source of children's educational material for miles around. Who is likely to respond to this? How can they be contacted? It is only when you have thought these questions through that you can plan your publicity campaign.

There are several different ways of getting publicity. The trick, if there is one, is using the method which will be seen by those you are trying to reach, and in a form which catches their imagination. The most usual forms of publicity for museum shops, are posters, leaflets, editorial coverage in the press and magazines, mentions on television and radio, and newspaper advertisements. It is generally better to spend your resources on getting editorial coverage in the media rather than paying for advertising, because people read the editorial content of a newspaper or magazine more closely than they read advertisements. Whilst it is cheaper to get editorial coverage rather

61

than pay for advertising, it is not without costs, most notably staff time, but also photocopying (or printing) of the press release, and postage. When preparing press releases follow the few golden rules – double spacing, clear headline, interesting first sentence, and a contact name and telephone number (office and home) for further information.

Work with colleagues in the musuem to link in promotions in the shop with events in the museum such as special exhibitions. Find out if any special groups of visitors are expected, for example, apart from school parties, groups from abroad, or special interest group. Why not send a postcard to the group leader suggesting a visit to the shop, perhaps even giving a special discount to the group. Make sure, when the museum's main publicity is being prepared, that the shop's existence is mentioned.

Make sure that the image of the shop you are trying to promote is a true reflection of the shopper's experience. Make your publicity material eye-catching, but not misleading. You may trick a journalist into publishing a less than accurate story once, but they never forgive or forget, and you can, in effect, end up on a black-list.

Organising a special promotion for a museum shop
Sue Runyard, *Press Officer, Natural History Museum*

On a hot July day, a perspiring van driver turned to me from loading up with giant taffeta and lace Christmas crackers, and asked 'I suppose you want me to dress up as Father Christmas too?' Of course – why didn't I think of that?

Timing on promotional matters is always important, but never more so than when dealing with the press. For most museum shops the family audience is crucial, and any favourable mentions of their products in the women's magazines proves profitable. Most of these magazines plan their issues very far in advance of publication. Therefore, for many of them during July and August the Christmas issues are being laid out, and during the lead-up to the Festive Season, Easter is on their mind. This has to be taken into account when sending samples of goods to shopping editors – always accompanied by price lists and photographs of course. National and local newspapers as well as some of the colour magazines need quite different time scales, and should be contacted during October and November.

Whenever sending sample products to journalists, it is vital to present your wares in a way which says something about your particular museum and your style of product, whether this means tying a carrier bag with an eye-catching ribbon, or decorating a box with appropriate motifs. Shopping editors are always on the look-out for colourful or unusual products, so the small capital outlay of sample presentations, backed up by follow-up work in checking that the recipient has everything required to write about your products, is a good investment if enthusiastically and thoughtfully carried out.

Apart from direct approaches to the press, there are many other ways to attract attention to museum shops. Few of us have generous funds for advertising, but we can more than compensate by ingenuity. Any promotion is bound to be product-based. There is no reason for the customer to enter a shop of any kind unless an attractive array entices them. An individual feature or characteristic can get you known, and can become an incentive to visit the museum itself. If your shop is known to sell the cheapest, prettiest or only version of one particular product, or to have the most representative and attractive array of charity Christmas cards, or the best selection of books on a given topic, this one characteristic alone can

63

be enough to draw people in. It also gives the opportunity to promote the shop on the basis of one product or one range of products, instead of selling the shop and its goods collectively, which in marketing and advertising terms needs greater saturation of effort. Perhaps we could learn from the loss-leader principle of supermarkets. A customer drawn in to search out a particular item is easily interested in others.

It is upon this basis that many book signings can prove successful – even by modestly well-known authors. Often the publisher of the book in question will be only too happy to help publicise the event, and the local newspaper will be prepared to carry advance notice. Book signings can bring in an interesting section of the local populace, often these are people who will make repeat visits once given the introduction. It is important to organise practical aspects well in advance, including the siting of the table or desk; allowing time for some copies of the book to be signed beforehand for sale during and after the session; and thanking the author properly afterwards, with a lunch or drink. After all, if successful, you may want a repeat performance.

Every opportunity should be taken to base promotions on special events or exhibitions occurring in the gallery programme. In this way there is a 'pick-a-back' effect from the main publicity attraction. If it is a Japanese exhibition, why not organise a demonstration of gift wrapping or origami? If a local craft is involved, why not organise a demonstration? If space is limited, see whether a competition or quiz can be linked in with an exhibition or education programme. Purchase of an item from the museum shop may be the way of qualifying for an entry form. If a well-known personality is due to open an exhibition, try to obtain a photograph of said person together with photographable shop product, whether a cuddly toy or replica. It may be used by the press in preference to any number of formal handshakes.

Opportunism and timing will always be the key, but understanding what fascinates people will help enormously. The only time I have known the Victoria & Albert Museum to close its doors through reasons of over-crowding was when we organised demonstrations by craftsmen throughout the galleries in 'The Makers' exhibition. People love seeing how things are made. Maybe there are products in your shop which could spark off ideas for weekend demonstrations – carefully planned and located to keep the traffic moving, and related to a museum exhibit which will reinforce the experience.

The success of the shops and the success of the museum are so intermingled that you may find it possible to 'borrow' display, poster or banner sites from time to time from the museum's own budget. These can be used to promote your wares. Don't overlook some of your outstanding advantages either. If you open on a Sunday (and perhaps have a museum restaurant or cafeteria near at hand), you are offering a service which may be unusual for the area or offer something in addition to a normal shopping expedition. This can be promoted as an asset for the whole museum.

One under-exploited area for promotion is the lack of joint schemes between museums with similar or compatible interests. Joint promotional leaflets or mail order schemes may be a way of sharing markets or economising on outlay. Whereas it may be difficult for one museum to mount a champagne reception to launch a range of products to journalists, a joint effort with equal participation can provide a pleasurable and successful occasion, while bringing costs down. Many newspapers and magazines try to provide a round-up or survey of museum shopping for Christmas or when looking at available replicas. It always involves numerous telephone calls and sometimes fruitless requests for photographs. Any combined effort to present our services jointly would yield a thankful response from that quarter. I have never seen any aspect of our public activity as being 'in competition'. One happy museum customer clutching a package of souvenirs is even more likely to try another museum next weekend.

Shop design and layout

Location

The first question for any museum shop is where should it be sited. The location of the shop is very important. Ideally the shop will be sited near the entrance, in the entrance hall, where it will be seen by all visitors. You want your shop entrance to be in the most heavily trafficked area (the one through which all visitors pass). In practice, there may be very little choice of location. The museum may have been built decades, if not centuries, before the possibility of a shop was even considered, and the building with its grand facade and wide promenades may not lend itself very readily to adaptation. (Often the building is so valued in its own right that any suggestion for adaption is seen as vandalism.) But it is surprising how space can be found for a shop; often the provision of cloakrooms, nearly always in a prime site by the entrance, was very lavish, and the cloakroom, or the best part of it, can be changed into a shop. This was the solution chosen, for example, at the Whitworth Art Gallery in Manchester. At the Natural History Museum alcoves on either side of a grand corridor have been converted into shops, in an ideal site on the left of the museum entrance, so the shops are not too intrusive, whilst being accessible to all visitors. The new shop at the Victoria and Albert Museum has been similarly sited to one side of the entrance, and this must be regarded as a very suitable location.

At National Trust shops the trend is to site the shops outside the main house – say in stables or purpose built outbuildings. The advantages of siting a shop outside the house are enumerated by the Trust as eliminating the inappropriate intrusion of retailing; there is less restriction on space, both for shop and stockrooms; deliveries do not have to be made during house opening hours and there are no problems of access for delivery; the shop can be open when the museum or house is not and lastly, the customers are free to enter the shop without paying admission charges. Nearly all these advantages

66

will be recognised as relevant by those running museum shops. The inappropriate intrusion of retailing will carry especial weight with those trading at religious sites (such as cathedrals) and many, such as Canterbury Cathedral, have found that a shop in the Cathedral precincts rather than the Cathedral gives all the advantages of still remaining highly visible and accessible whilst getting the money lenders out of the Temple. The great disadvantage of the shop being sited outside the museum is that visitors can by-pass it. When the shop at Killerton House, a National Trust house in Devon, was moved from the entrance hall to the stables, the percentage of visitors buying at the shop dropped from 55% to 38% (but the plan was that higher spending per capita would compensate for the fall in the number of customers).

It is not usually a choice between a cramped shop in the main museum, or a more spacious site elsewhere, but rather the cramped space in prime location versus slightly more space at the back or in the bowels of the building. Each site has to be judged on its merits, but on balance it is usually better to be crowded into a small space, rather than away from the main visitor traffic. The Science Museum in London found its trade virtually halved when it moved from its undoubtedly cramped shop just by the entrance to a less prominent site. This need not be the case though, as it may be worth putting a great deal of effort into better sign-posting to the shop, making the entrance to it enticing, etc., and hoping to benefit from the enlarged selling space. The Smithsonian Institute in Washington – at its largest museum shop, at the Museum of American Life – did just that, and after their initial trauma, have found that they have been able to develop a huge shop, with enormous range of goods, that certainly entices the visitor to spend once they have climbed the stairs down into it. (And clever use of glass opens up the shop from the staircase.)

It is generally better for trade if all visitors are not channelled through the shop either on their way in, or more usually, out of the museum. For example, at the Royal Horticultural Society shop at Wisley, the newly designed shop was unbearably overcrowded because all visitors were forced to pass through it, and similarly, the press of people channelled through the shop at the Jorvik Centre in York made it impossible for any customer to see the stock, let alone browse in a quiet pleasant atmosphere. What was planned as a cunning device to make sure every visitor went to the shop has rebounded – because it simply turns the shop into a crowded thoroughfare and those wanting to buy are unable to see the goods. The natural inclination is to try to get out of the overcrowded shop as quickly as possible. Channelling everyone through the shop, and the resultant overcrowding, also creates opportunities for the shoplifter. In the mêlée it is easy to slip things unobserved into pockets or bags. Also the two exits give opportunity of leaving without paying (one simply pockets the goods and goes back into the exhibition area, saying if challenged, that one is going back to look at something; once in the galleries the stolen item can be secreted more securely, and a brazen walk through the shop made subsequently). At the old shop at the Victoria & Albert Museum this was a favourite trick for shoplifters and one difficult to check.

The entrance hall may seem the most obviously desirable position for the shop, but consider other areas of the building in which people pass. True, everyone enters at the main hall, but do they also all walk up the main staircase, pass along all galleries and leave through a designated door. Observe the traffic flow carefully – and see if there is not an area en route that could be used as a shop. Do not choose a space just because it is available, if no visitors are likely to pass by. You may be forced to use the only available space which is away from highly trafficked areas but do not choose it because it has a nice lobby off it which would make you a comfortable office.

Wherever your shop is located try to give it a distinct entrance and specific physical area. It is a mistake to plonk down shelving in the hallway, with a few display cabinets and a till at one end. Studies on how customers act in shops show that people buy less, and browse less where there is space behind their backs. This is no doubt a very atavistic reaction, rooted in man's need to be able to defend himself, but, since it stops people buying, take note of it. Shops in enclosed spaces, which means walls or screens, not necessarily all to ceiling height, do better than those without. At the Tank Museum at Bovington, the fourth wall of the shop, dividing it from the main hall, is made up of large plants, in containers that can be moved out to enlarge the shop. This method of screening off the shop, whilst giving it a distinct area, makes the shop highly visible to those outside. Define the area of your shop, with a distinct entrance or perhaps a change in flooring, for example, by carpeting the shop floor; people entering the shop are psychologically prepared, virtually committed, to buying. Having a distinct shop gives that

68

psychological preparation. Does it deter people who might otherwise buy on impulse – almost certainly not. Since nearly all buying at the museum shop is for non-essential goods, bought in an unplanned manner, those who choose not to enter the shop to be tempted are unlikely to be tempted if they were in the shop! Some people enjoy shopping and others hate it – it is the latter who will not bother to visit the shop. The entrance must be inviting. It must entice the customer in, and suggest that the shop will be worth a visit. Like the display windows of department stores the entrance, and view through it, must tempt the customer, but also relate to the actual experience you are offering. It is no good having an entrance with showcases dressed like a display for Liberty's oriental department, if all you are selling are key fobs, postcards and catalogues. The style of your entrance must reflect the style of your shop.

Principles of shop design

When designing your shop go back to first principles. Nearly all shops are derivative – that is, they look like other shops. Of course you want your shop to be recognisable as a shop, and you want your customers to feel comfortable shopping in it. Firstly, let us consider what you want of your shop in physical terms. The shop must be an area in which to display merchandise to advantage; where the prospective customer can see and handle, the stock; an area that is physically comfortable for both customer and shop staff (so they all feel cheerful and that will help sales). As a museum shop you would, or should, want the shop to continue the experience of the museum, and have some of its atmosphere. This too will influence the shop's layout. There are certain physical conditions that are essential to achieve the shop's basic functions, as listed above. Firstly, keep the aisles wide, so shoppers are not jostled whilst they browse, nor made to feel uncomfortably crowded. There is always a temptation to make the display tables or counters too wide and the aisles too narrow. Do not do this – the customers will show their dissatisfaction by buying less. Remember that many of your visitors are families and a mother with a crush of children takes up a good deal of aisle space. You can reduce aisle space in the peripheral areas of the shop, where traffic is lower; in fact widening and narrowing the aisles is a way of imposing traffic (customer) flow. You may want to keep all but serious customers from leafing through your expensive art books and can do this partly by narrowing the aisles by the art book shelves.

Lighting

Lighting is a very important factor in determining the success of a shop. It is not enough to be simply well lit. The style of lighting will influence customer behaviour. Lighting has a subliminal effect on behaviour. Fluorescent, high intensity, non-directional light, such as is used in supermarkets, is associated by customers with low prices. Incandescent illumination is associated with exclusivity, and therefore higher prices. 'Full spectrum' lighting gives natural colour and should be used where possible. Spotlights should be used to focus attention on merchandise – people's attention is drawn to the lightest spot in the room, so make sure that your featured merchandise is highlighted (literally). Try to have a flexible lighting system, so you can focus on different parts of the shop, depending on which area you are highlighting. Lighting is also to do with customer comfort (if the customers are comfortable they are more likely to browse and buy). A great many museum shops are very poorly lit. Sometimes in old buildings where there is insufficient mains electricity, or no power points available, then the problems are very daunting – but make sure you are making the best of what you do have – consult a lighting specialist. If you are lucky enough to have natural light think about using your windows to add to the style of the shop. Plain plate glass may be too stark, and detract from the atmosphere you are striving for. Simple arches for the tops of the windows (made out of hardboard or plywood) or white trellis for sides and an arch at the top, are inexpensive but effective treatments. The colour of the shop walls are not likely to be particularly intrusive, since most of the walls will be covered with merchandise, but note that white walls reflect the light most, but customers spend more time in shops with walls of a neutral colour – say cream or beige. Other aspects of basic shop design which have been examined by behavioural scientists, and are relevant to you in designing your shop, are that floor contact is important for the customer's comfort and good humour – so carpet or soft, quiet flooring like cork is a good idea, also long aisles are psychologically disturbing (that is why in supermarkets or department stores, there are usually staggered displays to break up the aisles).

Shopfittings

Your shopfittings should be flexible. Whether you use conventional shop fittings or period furnishings it is essential that you can change the display around – not just adjust shelf heights, but change round the whole look of the shop. The Smithsonian Institute, which is the doyenne of museum trading, with around 15 shops at various sites, advocates changing the display in the museum shop every two weeks, and giving a total re-design and new look to each shop every two years. You might not feel as dynamic as that, but you should at least plan for change when buying any shop fittings, and buy units that give you flexibility. It is an awful inhibitant to change if you have to scrap all shop fittings and start from scratch. It may also be important to have free-standing units if your museum building is old, because you cannot expect to drill holes into fifteenth or sixteenth century buildings. In retailing generally the norm is now free-standing units (because they allow flexibility) and it is also possible to have lighting as an integral part of each display, all running off one power point. This is important in older buildings where power points are in short supply.

Museum shops are rarely designed by people who are specialists. Either the architect, who knows nothing about retailing, designs the shop along with the museum, or shopfitters are called in who know about bookshops or gift shops or supermarkets, but little about museum shops. Worst of all, the local authority or government department insists on your using their building works team, who are wonderful at designing and fitting offices, but completely inexperienced in matters of retailing. There are specialist shopfitters who could design a perfectly good museum shop, but unfortunately very few have ever been given the chance. If your funds will extend to it, and you are starting from scratch you should walk round a trendy shopping area like Covent Garden, choose a shop whose overall appearance you like, and ask them who designed and fitted out the shop. It is very unlikely that you will have enough freedom of funding to do this, so at least try to work with whoever will be either designing the shop, or if you do not have a designer, directly with the carpenter, or shopfitter, and give them clear instructions as to what you want. Tell them from the start the system must be flexible. Try to use standard components rather than having to have everything custom built. There are lots of shop fittings on the market, you can trace the suppliers through trade catalogues, at Trade Shows or through the Yellow Pages. Shopfitters can be very knowledgeable about shop design and planning, cogniscent of the latest research, they can help you foresee problems and overcome them, but they can also be simply fitting installers, skilled tradesmen who do not regard it as their business to know about focusing merchandise. They will tend to regard shop fitting and storage rather like a fitted wardrobe, a simple problem of shelf space. Be aware of what type of shopfitter you are employing. Brief both fully, but be particularly cautious in leaving anything to the discretion of the latter. (A parallel can be drawn with printing − never let a printer be a designer). Drawn on the expertise of the display department of your leading department stores. They have to know about shop layout, it is the cornerstone of their trade. People are flattered to be asked to help, and you are more likely to receive help than a refusal.

It will be cheaper to use standard components rather than have to have all units purpose built, and there are a large number of different types of fittings. You may want a 'hi-tech' look, say if you are a gallery with a great deal of modern art, and so could use systems with wire grids and wire baskets and shelves which can be hung on the wall grids (these can be coloured or plain). You may want a more mellow, country-style, in which case choose natural wood. There are very good systems, rather like Remploy's Lundia range, which have open wooden uprights with dowels, into which cupboards and shelves can be fitted. There are metal bracket systems which clip on to metal strips in the wall − shelves and square bins can be slotted into the system. You can now get perspex systems, particularly for displaying cards and stationery items. Perspex is used in conjunction with wood or 'formica' type board. The most prevalent shop fittings are those made totally of 'formica' (or usually a cheaper substitute), generally in white. These are relatively inexpensive but wear badly − the veneered boards are likely to chip at the edges. The plastic surfaces are functional and set the tone of the shop as nearer to a supermarket than a high quality gift shop.

Whatever type of fitting you choose, you can also use to great advantage pieces of furniture such as kitchen dressers, or sideboards, or old library shelves. These items of furniture help set the scene in your shop. It is interesting that in a shop which is actually displaying 90% of its merchandise on conventional shopfittings, yet has a display of goods on a kitchen dresser, and bowls of dried flowers on the windowsills, the customers when asked to recall the shop and its type of shopfittings will remember these features, because they set the tone for the shop. You may even set a price on the furniture! Try to make your shop memorable, but remember your shop fittings must be functional not just beautiful. (It is said that a shop fitting can do everything a salesperson can do, except take the money!)

When planning your shop layout consider your available space. One thing to consider is height. Often when the shop is a screened-off area of a high hall or corridor, you will find that the shop does not have a ceiling. This is uncomfortable for shoppers — rather like open space behind their backs — it also tends to give a noise problem, as the noise is echoed. It is better to put a false, noise absorbant ceiling on the shop than leave it open. If your funds run to it why not make a feature of the ceiling, with a modest dome effect, perhaps achieved by draping fabric (be careful of the fire hazard). Where space permits you could even introduce a mezzanine floor, or a gallery. A spiral staircase, always an interesting architectural feature, can be sited at the corner of the shop, or even in the centre as at the Royal Academy's shop. You do not want hordes of customers clattering up and down a spiral staircase but you could use the mezzanine for offices (as at the Royal Academy) or create a gallery and display higher-priced items, such as high-value art books or facsimiles, which the serious customer is likely to bother to go up and see. Make sure your signposting indicates that the goods are on view in the gallery. Offer to bring the items down for any disabled or elderly person unable to manage the stairs.

Remember when designing the shop to provide for storage. You need to have, in the shop, enough to enable you to restock during the day. The main stock-room may be some distance away from the shop, and it will be difficult for staff to leave the shop unattended or understaffed, whilst they trundle goods in, so try to ensure you have

73

at least enough stock on hand to top up your stock throughout the day. You do not need the same amount of back-up stock for each item, as some will sell more quickly than others. Be sensible about it. Have cupboards, or drawers at the bottom of all display counters. Keep the stock in them tidily, in an order pre-determined and agreed by all the staff, and re-stock from the main store if necessary every day, ideally before opening time, or during the first quiet hour. If you are using tables in a central island, if storage space is at a premium, cover the tables with green baize to the floor, and store goods under the table. If you are concerned about the security (someone walking off with the boxes) then buy a metal security cage to fit the space. Remember, in your storage space you should fit, as well as stock, spare bags, till rolls, spare light bulbs, cloths for clearing up spills, and spare rolls for the pricing gun!

The number of staff running the shop, and the number of entrances (hopefully only one) will determine where you site the till. You want the till to be near the exit, but not too obtrusive – it should not be the main focus of the shop (you want the customers to look at the merchandise, not be reminded of the till!). If you have only one member of staff in the shop then it is important that they can see the entire shop from the till. Some shop designers place the till on a central circular counter, the staff standing on a raised dais. This helps visibility, but the shop assistant is imprisoned in the central unit, and it also makes them seem too remote from the customers. It is not conducive to the friendly atmosphere of the shop – it is rather a defensive stand against marauding school parties! The till has to be kept secure (it should be screwed down) and should not be left unattended if the shop is busy (if it is remember to immobilise it by removing the key). If the shop is staffed generally only by one person (which is not ideal, but may be the case) then the shop design must take this into account, not only by being particularly easily visible, but because that member of staff has to be able to move very easily and quickly round the shop, tidying and filling shelves, putting up displays, answering questions and taking the money. Your shop has to be designed for your staffing level, it is no good having a wonderful looking shop that you cannot actually maintain, because you do not have sufficient staff, nor is it any good having a shop which needs a window dresser to keep it looking nice if you do not have one permanently on your staff. Your display units should be fool proof, literally.

Grouping merchandise

Your display units are flexible, your shop well lit, the aisles nice and wide, the floor carpeted, the ceiling sound-proofed; how are you going to layout your merchandise? What you are trying to do in your shop design is tempt the customer into the shop; make it easy for him to find what he is interested in; group products so he can find a range of related items, and make it easy for the customer to make the purchase. However small your shop it helps to subdivide it visually, and create separate displays. Your shop layout must be comprehensible to the shopper. It is no good grouping products by some subtle index system determined by the manageress for ease of re-ordering. A customer will not bother to search out items, if they feel 'lost' in your shop they will leave it. Everyone has expectations as to how shops will work, and although this allows for an enormous range of variations, by and large successful shops will try to fit in with these general rules. To illustrate the point from everyday experience, in a book shop books may be grouped by subject in fairly broad categories; within those categories they may be arranged by alphabetical order either of title or author. Imagine a bookshop where books were arranged by jacket colour. What customer could be bothered to search through the shelves looking for the titles he might be interested in. The shop must be 'easy to shop'.

You can either group products by type of product – all books together, all mugs and chinaware together, all tea-towels together, or you may categorise items by subject so, for example, all items on Romans are together, as are those on Impressionist painters, or traditional handicrafts. You may decide to group things on the basis of their likely customers, most usually all children's items, or inexpensive items, in one section. Whatever categorisation you use make sure it seems logical to the customer. Most probably you will want to use all three methods of organising your merchandise, and it might be that in conjunction with displays of like objects, you will have features or 'themes' drawing together items relevant to a particular collection in the museum. This means that you may well have the same item displayed in different parts of your shop, because the customer may go to the sections he thinks he is interested in, and overlook merchandise in other sections – by making a special display of related items you draw his attention to an additional range of products.

The amount of space you give to each item should relate to your expected sales levels. You should give most space, in the best position, to items that sell best. In any shop 80% of your turnover will usually come from 20% of your 'lines' (the different items you stock). By featuring these items, and displaying them in the best position you will make most money – because a small percentage increase in sales of these items will give a great deal in profit terms. The best display position is at eye level, within arm's reach; people reach out and touch, and subsequently, buy items displayed at eye level. Put your best selling items at this level – you may want to continue the display vertically – it is easier for the eye to travel vertically than horizontally. If the best selling items get the best display position are you not lessening the chances of the slower selling items improving their performance? Whilst changing position will help sales, it will help fast selling lines sell even faster, and so you will do even better. Monitor the performances of your items, every week, and see which positions in your shop are best. Give the most space, not just the best position, to the most profitable items. You can put your 'basic demand lines', those items which are steady, moderate sellers which people expect to find in the shop in the second best selling positions. These items are the backbone of your trade; they need to be visible, so customers can find them without searching, but do not warrant the star treatment of fast selling lines.

Slow selling lines can be relegated to the worst positions; the darkest corners, the lowest shelves. Of course, any item in this position will perform poorly, so make sure that you have tried the item out in a better position. (No one buys items expecting them to be bad sellers, except for window dressing purposes or a sense of obligation when it comes to specialist books) so try all new lines out, and be quick to reposition as necessary, ideally working on a two week testing period.

Recognise that some items will sell better at certain times of the year, and re-position accordingly, for example, increasing the display space of children's items to coincide with school holidays (if that is when you have most children in the shop). Set up special displays to coincide with exhibitions, and give them prominence; remember, stock bought in for the exhibition needs to be sold whilst the exhibition is on – its chances of selling afterwards are very poor. You may try to devise interesting and appropriate ways of displaying goods for a special exhibition – for example, a temporary pagoda for a Japanese exhibition or a gazebo for a garden exhibition. Do not be over-ornate. You are trying to run a shop, not build a theatre set, but do try to enter into the spirit of things!

Show your faith in your merchandise by buying sufficient of any item to give it impact. People look at piled up items and seeing a great many items makes them feel they might want one (after all, they reason, the retailer clearly expects a lot of people to want them). American museum shops are much better at piling their merchandise, to give impact. For example, it is interesting to contrast the display of the catalogue for the Chagall exhibition that was shown at the Royal Academy in London and the Museum of Fine Art, Philadelphia. At the Royal Academy the catalogues were displayed at the exhibition entrance and in the shop in piles of around a dozen. At Philadelphia the entire stock of catalogues, literally thousands, were stacked, as they would be in a store room, only unwrapped, in the window embrasures. The impact was enormous – it gave every visitor the hidden message that they were expected to buy a catalogue (else why would the museum have so many in stock?). Of course, space is at a premium, and most museum shops would find it hard to give over space to a display of three thousand catalogues – but in fact the display because it was piled so high, was quite compact, and those catalogues would have been taking up space in a store room. It is better to restrict the number of lines, and give in depth promotion to those you have. (This does not mean over-order slow selling lines, but that after testing a small quantity you can then re-order in sufficient amounts to give a display with impact).

Use signs in your shop to indicate sections (such as postcards, local history, museum catalogues) and map the shop out for customers. Also use signs to explain the merchandise – if it is replicas, by describing what the original item was, where it was found, and what the replica is made of, and if it is in a limited edition. These 'provenance' cards give an added importance and interest to the product, and involve the customer. You may decide to give provenance cards with replicas, but other items can also benefit from descriptive signs – maybe explaining (not justifying!) why the item has been chosen for the shop. For example, you may have signs above jars of honey, describing how honey has been a traditional product in the area over centuries, that the first recorded hives were kept by

77

monks in the 11th century, but local records show Romans in the area ate honey. Explain where the honey you stock is produced, if it is local, and mention any other attractive selling feature (for example, that it is made in the traditional manner).

Ideally, you will think of your shop as a stage set. You will take care to view it as an outsider would, going round to the front of the counter to see the display and entrance from the customer's point of view. You will want to make your shop fun to shop in; displaying your stock to advantage, and making customer and staff alike cheerful because the place is fun to be in.

Summary

The shop's location is important. Make it easy and comfortable for visitors to shop in your shop. Keep your fittings flexible. Keep the shop well lit. Feature new merchandise. Put fast selling stock in the best display position. Change the display and layout to maintain interest.

Catering for tourists in the museum shop.
Joanna Dodsworth, *Bodleian Library, Oxford.*

Tourists are very important to the Bodleian Library's shop. From March to October 95% of our customers are tourists (both foreign and English). An increasing number of low-season package tours bring us a trickle of foreign visitors throughout the year, and of course, many of those using the Library are foreign academics who will buy small gifts and cards to take home. We find our tourist customers spend more on average than our readers and Oxford residents.

Our tourists come mostly in coach loads, and are given very little time by their tour-leaders and guides to spend in the building so we keep the tourist 'Oxford Views' postcards, guide books and small souvenir items at the entrance to the shop and near the till. Try to see that tourist items are as far as possible self-service, and in a pack. It is very time-wasting for shop staff to have to fold things up or put it into special bags. Posters and prints can be sold already rolled up into a clear plastic tube; a pack of ten popular postcards saves agonizing, and sells more cards per customer. But if yours is the sort of museum where people come to spend several hours, it may be a good idea to place the popular postcards further into the shop, but of course clearly visible from the entrance, to make the customer walk past displays of the more expensive items.

You must get to know what kind of tourist is coming into your shop. In the Bodleian Library we have found we have to stock some general Oxford souvenirs and guide books, because many of our tourists do not stop anywhere else in Oxford. But for those others who are spending some days in the City, we keep exclusive Bodleian Library things for them to buy as a change from the standard leather bookmarks and tee shirts sold in every department store in Oxford; for example, we sell book-plates using medieval woodcuts, actually printed in the Library; and the mass-produced leather bookmarks are designed specially for us, based on decorative bookbindings in the library's collection.

When selecting stock the most important thing to remember is portability and packaging. It may seem obvious, but it is surprising how many otherwise attractive souvenir items fail on this point. Foreign tourists are touring – they want to take back things that are light, unbreakable, and not too bulky, as well as being local, typical, and preferably useful as well as being attractive.

79

Our tourists do not buy books, except of course for guide books, which they buy eagerly; they tend to buy one guide book from a choice of about five we stock. They also buy very small books, so in our shop, visited by many coach parties of foreign tourists stopping off in Oxford on a day trip from London to Stratford, we have found that 'The Oxford Learner's Pocket Dictionary' and the 'Oxford Mini Dictionary' in their colourful OUP dictionary livery sell excellently, as do the V & A's reprint of a book of manners for children.

There is no need to try to find staff who are linguists – school French is no help with a coach full of Korean businessmen. But when you are selecting staff, you should bear in mind that the most important asset in dealing with foreign tourists is patience and a liking for people, and for helping them, as well as the great virtue of being able to keep your head. Museum shop staff must be able to keep their head when confronted with thirty people each waving a £10 note and wanting to buy one postcard at 15p and to remain courteous and unflappable.

However, staff may have to be discouraged from being too help-ful. Ten minutes could be spent explaining the way to the Post Office to just one of a crowd of tourists, who, having selected a postcard nearly always wants to buy a stamp as well and then find a post box, to the greater annoyance and irritation of the rest.

We have in fact found that a stamp-vending machine in the shop is worth its weight in gold. The shop makes no profit on the stamps (they are bought in at cost) but it saves a great deal of staff time explaining where the nearest Post Office is.

If possible, try to supply a basic guide in some languages other than English, even if it is a simple leaflet giving a translation to be tucked into the glossy colour guide book. But it is very difficult to decide which are the essential languages after French and Italian; German, Dutch and Scandinavian tourists all seem to have at least some, and often excellent, English, and outside Europe so do the Japanese.

Usually we bring out our Christmas stock for the local Oxford buyers in October – but recently we have started to put out Christ-mas cards in July. Among the large number of American University and other summer school students in Oxford during the Summer vacation as well as in the coach parties, there are many who like to take back Christmas cards and small Christmas gifts that they cannot get back home.

Financial Information and Control

The accounting and financial management of the museum's trading company is an integral part of its work, and should be understood by those involved in the trading operation. There is no room for staff who boast 'I don't understand figures, I leave it all to the account-ant!', because they are admitting that they do not understand, nor believe it necessary for them to understand, a very fundamental aspect of the whole work. Clearly not all the staff need the same degree of financial acumen; but all must accept firstly, the need to keep accurate financial and stock records (just as they would all accept that they should keep records of correspondence), and secondly, that the trading activity costs and earns money and is not to be carried on without considering the financial implications.

Every company has to keep accurate financial records and produce audited annual accounts. In addition, if you are registered for VAT you must keep accurate records to enable you to do your VAT returns. It is possible for the staff of the trading company to keep virtually no records and simply hand a miscellany of assorted cheque stubs, receipts, paid and unpaid bills, and bank statements to their accountant and let him sort it out. There are two main drawbacks to this behaviour – the first and minor one, is that you are paying the accountant about £30 an hour to do your filing; and secondly, you are not keeping any financial records which could be of use to you in judging how your trading activities are in fact progressing. You should not keep accounts simply to satisfy the annual auditor, they should be providing you with crucial information on all aspects of your work. At the most basic level the accounts will tell you what you have spent, and what you have earned. They should also show what is selling well and what is selling slowly. The accounts provide the basis of stock control, and tell you when to re-order. From the accounts you can work out which days of the week and months of the year are best for trade; you can work out your likely percentage of bad debts; you can compare prices from suppliers over a period of time and judge whether you are putting up your prices quickly enough to meet rising costs.

What financial records are you going to keep?

Think hard about what information you would like, and organise your accounts so that you can retrieve the information accordingly. The local authority or other funding bodies may also have specific requirements. Whatever the organisation or company, it is likely to keep a Cash Analysis Book, with income listed on the left hand page and expenditure on the right. Within this basic framework you can organise your information as you like. It is usually very helpful to discuss with your accountant, or finance officer, and your staff what might be useful categories in which to break down the information. Typical column headings on the expenditure side will be Date; Details; Totals; Total net of VAT; VAT; Cheque or warrant number; salaries (including pensions); rent/rates; occupancy overheads (electricity, gas, insurance); postage; telephone; stock purchase (this may be subdivided into books, own originated products, other suppliers etc.); travel. On the income side you may simply lump together all shop sales, then have categories for sales to other museums, and mail order. Or you may separate books and publications on which you do not charge VAT and gift and souvenir items on which you do. You can categorise in any way you find useful. Since you are likely to subtotal the categories to give running totals, it makes sense to categorise items you want to keep a watch on, without having to re-analyse the columns. Remember, you can always change the categories, once a week if you like, all you have to do is turn over a page! There is to most people something very daunting about the pristine columns of an accounts book; they hate crossings out, but it is more important to get your information down in the form most useful to you than to preserve a neat book (and anyway, the auditor scribbles all over the book as he cross-checks the figures!)

Apart from your Cash Analysis Book you will probably have subsidiary record books. It is usually sensible to keep a Purchase Day Book, which lists all orders from the organisation. This is a very useful check on the rate at which funds are being spent, and usually means that a proper authorisation procedure is put into action so that people are not just ordering items without either the responsibility of working within an agreed budget, or informing the finance officer that the money has been committed. The Purchase Day Book is the cornerstone of your method of accounting for your purchases. It should be used in conjunction with a strict procedure for all purchasing. All orders should be in writing, and signed by an authorised person. It helps if each section of the expenditure budget is the responsibility of one person, or department, so that one person becomes responsible for seeing that the budget is not overspent. (If there are substantial increases in any prices you may have to re-examine and adjust your whole budget). All orders should show the price, so that when the invoice is received for the goods you can verify that the correct quantity has been supplied, at the agreed price. Remember to mark invoices paid (not only does this stop you inadvertently paying the same bill twice, it also prevents the invoice being used to support a fraudulent payment). Where there are substantial purchases from regular suppliers than it is usual to keep a 'Purchase Ledger' in which the accounts with each supplier are listed, and these are kept in the mysterious double entry system!

Sales can be recorded in a Sales Day Book (possibly in conjunction with a Sales Ledger analysing the sales by type or customer). Even the simplest modern till can, in fact, analyse sales figures for you, and these provide the basic figures for your Sales Day Book. Remember though that the till cannot guess the figures, it can simply record what it is directed to − and if the cashier does not press the right buttons, the figures will not be of use − either they will not be analysed by type of sale, or more usually they will be incorrectly recorded − for example, all lumped together as publications, or gifts. There is no use having a till that requires very sophisticated 'keying in' if your staff are under a great deal of pressure from clamorous coach parties or school groups, and even a simple system, with say 8 codes, can, and will, break down at times. If your turnover is high enough it may be worth training a cashier, because the analyses done at the point of sale will be such a considerable saving in time given to accounting and stock control subsequently.

VAT RULES FOR INVOICES AND CREDIT NOTES

1. Invoices

The Value Added Tax (General) Regulations 1980 require that a trader registered for VAT who makes a taxable supply to another taxable person must provide him with a tax invoice. The issue of a tax invoice in respect of a zero-rated supply is optional.

Except as indicated in the paragraph below,* a tax invoice must contain the following particulars:

- Identifying number and date of issue.
- Tax point (date of supply).
- Name, address and VAT registration number of the suppliers.
- Name and address of the person to whom the goods or services are supplied.
- Type of supply, i.e. sale; hire purchase; credit sale; conditional sale or similar transaction; loan; exchange; hire; lease or rental; process (i.e. goods made from customer's materials); sale on commission; or supply on sale or return or similar terms.
- Description sufficient to identify the goods or services supplied.
- Quantity of goods or extent of services and amount, excluding tax, payable for each description.
- Gross total amount payable excluding tax.
- Rate of any cash discount offered.
- Rate and amount of tax chargeable.

* For amounts not exceeding £50 (including tax), retailers and other taxable persons supplying goods and services direct to both the general public and other taxable persons may issue tax invoices showing the following particulars only:

- Name, address and registration number of the supplier.
- Tax point (date of supply).
- Description sufficient to identify the goods or services supplied.
- Total amount payable including tax.
- Rate of tax in force at time of supply.

VAT RULES FOR INVOICES AND CREDIT NOTES

2. Credit notes

In accordance with Customs and Excise requirements, a supplier who gives a customer a credit relating to taxable supplies for which a tax invoice was issued must issue a credit note showing the following particulars:

- Identifying number and date of issue.
- Supplier's name, address and VAT registration number.
- Customer's name and address.
- Reason for the credit (e.g. returned goods).
- Description sufficient to identify the goods or services for which credit is being allowed.
- Quantity and amount credited for each description.
- Total amount credited excluding VAT.
- Rate and amount of VAT credited.

The number and date of the original tax invoice must also be shown on the credit note, but if this is not possible the supplier must be able to satisfy Customs and Excise in some other way that he accounted for tax on the original supply.

If you are registered for VAT you will need a VAT book, listing all the sales on which you are charging VAT. (You may find that your cash register will keep duplicate till receipts, with records of all VAT-liable sales, and these can be filed and treated as a VAT book). You must keep all receipts for items on which you are claiming VAT inputs – if you do not the VAT man can disallow the claim. More of a deterrent is that his periodic visits will degenerate into a nightmare of an arithmetic lesson where you cannot get your sums right! You must also keep a list of credit notes, for the VAT man, if you are making refunds. The rules for VAT invoices and credit notes are set out in the table above.

Your Cash Analysis Book is your main record of all financial transactions. You may want to keep subsidiary books, with fuller information on particular categories, which you simply summarise in the main cash book. When the term book is used it does not have to be taken literally – you may find loose leaf files better. Whatever you find easiest to use you should use – do not be talked into using standard cash books which impose on you a method of keeping records you do not find useful.

Ideally, the keeping of the financial records is not hived off to a book-keeper. The head of the trading company will certainly not have the time to do all the books, but should be familiar with the summary position as outlined in the main Cash Analysis Book. It is no coincidence that in literature the rich misers are always shown huddled over their books – they grew rich by knowing their true financial position.

Management accounts

Once you have established an efficient method of recording financial information you can use the information to discover what has happened in the past, and, even more important, you can plan for the future. The main tool for the financial control of your trading is the budget – this is your financial plan for the coming year (though you may have a budget for any number of years ahead, most typically three or five yearly budgets). When drawing up the budget both staff and management have an opportunity to discuss and, hopefully, agree the plans for the coming year. Drawing up a budget is a time wasting exercise if once drawn up it is ignored. The budget should be used to monitor actual performance, and reasons for discrepancies against projected and real performance examined.

Your main budget shows the main categories of income and expenditure. It is your plan of what you hope will happen in the coming year. Firstly, you must decide how to categorise the different heads of income and expenditure. (These may very typically follow the headings you use in your Cash Analysis Book.) Under each heading you have to make assumptions on which to base your calculation of the likely costs of each item of expenditure, and estimate the likely amounts of income from each source. It is very important when drawing up the budget to show the basis of your assumptions (for example, are all costs based on last year + 10%?). Remember to allow for inflation, and that not all items are equally affected by inflation. Once you have drawn up the draft budget circulate your colleagues and invite their comments. Do your assumptions seem reasonable? Has anything been left out? Have you taken into account staff increments? Have you allowed for temporary staff in case of sickness, or maternity leave, or the cost of recruitment advertising if staff leave? It is prudent to be cautious when projecting likely sales, and to allow generously for unforeseen contingencies on the expenditure side, because then your actual performance against budget will be enhanced. Once you have drawn up the budget, and everyone involved has agreed the assumptions, you may have to act to change the situation the budget postulates. For example, you may be heading for a loss, because of plans to invest heavily in stock, such as own publications, which call for high initial outlay. What will you do? Will your museum agree to forego profits for a year, or perhaps longer? Perhaps they will ask that you show them a 5 year budget, which will indicate exactly when the shop will become profitable. You or your management committee may feel that the staff costs are too high for the projected turnover, and ask you to reduce them; they may feel allowance for the telephone is too high, and ask for that to be monitored.

The main income and expenditure budget should be used in conjunction with a cash flow budget, which attempts to forecast the flow of cash in and out of the company throughout the year, so that you can avoid the crisis that might be caused by a temporary shortfall. Remember that a shortfall, though temporary, can cause bankruptcy. If your cash flow budget shows a temporary shortfall you can arrange a temporary overdraft at the bank. The bank manager will, in effect, ask to see a cash flow budget before he grants overdraft facilities, and your having one prepared can only inspire confidence. Your cash flow budget may show that you are likely to have cash surpluses at certain times of the year (for example at the end of the summer season, or as a result of the pre-Christmas rush) and you should plan to invest the surplus, short term; from your cash flow budget you should be able to calculate for how long you can invest the money. To draw up a cash flow budget you divide all your categories of income and expenditure in your main budget, and ascribe them to the month in which the actual payments will be made, or income received. For example, your insurance premium is paid annually, so you assign it to the month in which it is due.

The cash flow budget allows you to plan. It eliminates management by hysteria, and by forward planning removes the crises which many people seem to enjoy (they believe it shows their artistic temperament!). Drawing up a cash flow budget will not overcome any of the periodic shortfalls it shows. It gives you time to plan your course of action. What can you do? Firstly, delay paying bills for as long as possible. Ask suppliers if you can have a longer time to pay (it may result in higher prices, but this may still be worth it). Make sure you have invoiced for any goods you have supplied, and send reminders to late payers – if necessary telephoning to remind them. Shortfalls in your cash-flow show you need to stimulate sales, which may be hard at times when visitors to the museum are scarce. Try to extend your season by organising special events, such as craft demonstrations, book signings, literary lunches, and visits by Father Christmas and the Easter Bunny! The activities generated by the shop, as part of its promotional programme, should be an intrinsic part of the museum's attempts to draw visitors, and act as a cultural focus in its community.

If after drawing up the income and expenditure and cash flow budgets you heave a sigh of relief and stick them in a drawer, then the value of the exercise is lost. You should use both throughout the year to monitor performance, and up-date the figures as necessary. Ideally you should each month reconcile the cash book with the bank statement, and produce a receipts and payments amount (that is a simple summary of all monies received and payments out). By taking into account monies owing, both to and by you, the receipts and payments account turns into an income and expenditure account. (These are technical terms used in accounting and book-keeping, and like printers' jargon it helps if you know the terminology). You may want to produce a balance sheet (that is a summary of assets and debts) either monthly, quarterly or half-yearly. Certainly if your trading operation is large enough to have a finance officer, even part-time, you may ask him as part of the financial information you need to work with (that is your management accounts) to prepare you a balance sheet as often as once a month. Like all financial information it is no good asking someone to prepare and update figures if you are not going to use them. You are not humouring the accountant by setting him little jobs; try to ask for the financial information you want. You will certainly want sales figures, broken down by category – what percentage of spending was on books and publications, what on postcards, film, gifts etc. What were the number of sales, and the average value of each sale. (This information should be easily gathered by using the till, because even the simplest £150 electronic

Cash flow budget – The Toyland Museum Shop

	Jan	Feb	Mar	Apr	May	June	July	Aug	Sept	Oct	Nov	Dec	Carried forward
Payments													
Salaries 31000	2500	2500	2500	2500	2500	2900*	2900*	2900*	2500	2500	2500	2500	
NI and Pension 6000	500	500	500	500	500	580	580	580	500	500	500	500	
Light and Heat 600		150†			150			150			150		£50
Telephone 720			180			130			230			180	
Post/Stationery/ Display 1250	600				500			600			150		
Insurance and Credit	600												
Publicity	400		450			800					150	650	
Stock													
Books 25,000	8000	1000	1000	6000	1000	1000	2000	1000	1000	1000	1000	1000	
Gifts 80,000	22000	3000	3000	20000	3000	3000	10000	3000	3000	4000	3000	3000	
Own publications 12,500	4500	–	–	2000	–	–	4000	–	–	1500	–	–	
Xmas special purchases 10,000	–	–	–	–	–	–	–	5000	5000	–	–	–	
Special exhibition purchases 20,000	–	–	10000	–	–	10000	–	–	–	–	–	–	

* temporary extra help
† £50 carried forward from previous year

89

till will produce this information automatically). You could then correlate number of sales with number of visitors to the museum.

When you have gathered all this information, which hopefully you are doing quite routinely, compare actual income and expenditure against budget, and make a note of any substantial discrepancies – and if relatively poor performance means you are going to be over-spent on budget, you must act, to cut expenditure or bolster income. If your sales levels are higher than planned this will have implications for your stock purchase budget – you may need to spend money on re-stocking. (This is not a decision that can be taken simply by looking at the budget – you cannot say, 'Oh, sales went up 30%, we need to spend 30% more on stock', you have to consider what made sales increase – was there a temporary exhibition which drew crowds, and were the increased sales all of the exhibition catalogue – in which case you do not need to restock).

One set of figures that cannot be derived from monitoring your own performance, is how it compares with other similar museum shops. The only way to find this out is by asking colleagues in other museums. Be very cautious of their answers – some inflate their performance, and in other cases you are not comparing like with like (as they may not take into account all overheads, they may pay high rent to the museum, or none, and may have free staff provided by the warders). But having said be cautious, it is still important to try to get some figures.

10 financial facts most useful to know about other museum shops

1. Spending per visitor (and number of visitors to museum).
2. Number of visitors buying at the shop.
3. Spending per customer (value of each sale).
4. Breakdown of spending by category (% on publications, gifts etc.)
5. Proportion of own products, bought-in products.
6. Turnover.
7. Net Profit.

8. Overall operating costs (and what this includes).
9. Staffing levels.
10. Earnings per linear foot of display.

Your management accounts are the tools you need to do your job well. It is very unlikely that you can operate successfully without having the financial information on which to base your decisions. Certainly the larger your turnover the more you will need a management accounting system. In the early days, often the museum's trading is so small that those involved know exactly what has sold, which lines are doing well, how much is in the till and what the average value of each purchase was. As the operation expands you cannot expect to keep the information in your head, and it is unreasonable to try (it is not some test of virility to do so) – apart from anything else that information needs to be shared with the rest of the staff. Try to make sure that the staff understand the accounts, or at least those aspects that relate specifically to their work. Give your staff training on financial understanding (either taking advantage of courses organised by outside bodies or hold an annual understanding the accounts training day). Above all involve them in the financial management of the company, and make them understand that the management accounts are telling a story, and it is the story of the performance of the trading company seen in one dimension, but a very important dimension, because the punch line is whether the trading company is flourishing or failing.

How to get capital

It is possible to start a business on the corner of a kitchen table with a good idea and £5 from the house-keeping. Museum trading, because of the need for a physical presence in the museum itself, even if it is not a full-blown shop, will involve some expenditure on minimal display fittings, a till and a range of stock, so you will need some capital. You may be able to get a great deal of stock without paying for it right away (through a variety of special deals ranging from sale or return, through long-term credit facilities to acting as a sales agent taking a commission of sales) but you would have a very lopsided range of goods for sale, if the main criterion for selection were the fact that you did not have to pay for it! So the first problem to address is how to get the capital to start your museum trading enterprise.

The variety of ways museums fund their trading is considerable. Most usually, local authority run museums will have a grant for the shop included in their overall budget. (This rarely allows for any expansion.) In government funded museums usually the trading enterprise is similarly included as an element in the museum's annual budget. In museums set up as charitable trusts (though also in some others) the trading company is separately constituted and covenants its profits to the parent museum – it usually borrows from the parent museum, but can use the banks as a source of funds. Some museums have more singular methods of raising capital. At the National Galleries of Scotland, the Merchants Fund is earmarked for that purpose. The Bodleian Library used the royalties on *Wind in the Willows* which it had been bequeathed by Kenneth Graeme. The Fitzwilliam Museum has to borrow from its parent body, the University of Cambridge, at commercial rates of interest.

If the museum is a registered charity or trust, then it is usual for the trading company to be funded by its parent charity. The museum has to have the powers in its trust deed to invest funds in this way, and either must charge a commercial rate of interest or, if it charges a lower rate, must do so in expectation of profits being earned of a sufficient level for it to be a good investment. As the trading company cannot retain any profits as working capital, it has to borrow from the parent museum at the beginning of each financial year. (Usually the trading company covenants, that is makes a binding commitment, to pay all profits to the museum, and so cannot retain profits. Were it to do so, the profits would be subject to corporation tax at whatever the prevailing level, and that is generally around 40%. If the parent museum cannot lend capital it still must be cheaper to borrow capital from the bank than to attempt to retain profits for re-investment.)

Local authority administered museums or those dependent on central government funding, face a variety of problems. One is that their budgets are liable to be raided when cuts are called for. Some museums have their budgets cut by the amount the trading company is estimated as likely to earn. Museums then feel they are being penalised for their initiative, and much acrimony ensues! (The

Government has recently promised that in future centrally-funded museums will be allowed to keep earnings.) If the museum's funding is cut by the trading company's expected profit, it is hard for the trading company to find the necessary capital for expansion. Its parent museum is probably unable to forego any of the trading profits to allow them to be set aside for re-investment. Some local authority run museums have made arrangements whereby any earnings can be earmarked for purchase or educational funds, and to protect this position against future raids, have drawn up a covenant accordingly. The trading company, whether it covenants its profits or has them absorbed into the local authority budget, still has the problem of getting capital. The local authority may draw up a budget which includes an element for stock purchase, but it is unlikely that this will be very generous – after all, faced with demands on funds for day centres, play schemes, or even the floral clock outside the Town Hall, how sympathetic would you be to the museum shop's demand for money for buying more stock, when they have a great deal of unsold stock from previous years?

A very common complaint from local authority and central government funded museums, where the Finance Officer holds sway, is that there is a belief that 'stock' is regarded as indivisible – that if the museum's trading company has £50,000 of back stock then based on its £20,000 a year sales, the Finance Officer thinks it has a good two years' stock. No account is taken of the fact that the stock is made up of the guide book, a catalogue from two past exhibitions, 6 postcards in the sepia and colour style of the 1930's and a range of slow selling books. Lucky the trading company that can persuade the auditors to 'write off' stock!

There is no answer, at least none that is likely to satisfy both sides, to the problem of fixing a satisfactory level of capital to fund new purchases or other expansion, such as display. At best, the competence of those running the shop will encourage those in charge of the funds to make the investment in expectation of a good return. It is easy to blame auditors for being excessively pernickety, and uncommercial, but the records probably point to years of poor trading results and levels of unsold, and unsaleable stock, much higher than would be tolerated in a small business with comparable turnover, where the owner was investing his own money. For a variety of reasons those responsible for museum trading operations have not always been as careful in spending the company's money as they might have been, and this has affected the treatment of their successors. There is blame on both sides. An auditor whose only concern is making sure all the postcards are counted and that stock is protected from customers, is not helpful in building up the trading to profitable levels. To resolve the problems inherent in the relationship between those in charge of funds (who want to save the money, not risk it) and the traders (who must have funds to enable them to trade) those involved must move from their position of traditional enemies, to that of allies. It needs patience, understanding of the problem of the other, and realisation that a different style of working is not necessarily wrong. The best chance of getting capital out of anyone – whether it is the Finance Officer, the Trustees or the Bank Manager, is to show how well you have performed in the past. The worst off is the new commercial manager whose predecessors have dissipated their inheritance, and who has to ask for funds on the basis of his competence!

Remember when asking for capital that the money could, if simply left on the money markets, earn interest of around 10%. Are you going to earn, after all expenses, substantially more than 10%? If not why should the money not be left in the bank, where it is not at risk. A little more humility in asking for other people's money to be put at risk as your trading company's capital, would probably be helpful in convincing those in charge of the money that you are aware of the problems. Always ask yourself, would you invest your own money in the museum's trading operation? If the answer is 'no' then why be surprised that other people feel the same way?

Summary

Those involved in trading must understand the financial implications. Accurate records must be kept. It is up to each trading company to decide how to keep its financial data, with ease of use a prime consideration. There are certain statutory obligations, and for VAT-registered companies, strict rules of procedure.

Use financial information to plan your operation – draw up a budget, and assess actual performance against budget. Use a cash flow budget to help plan purchases. Realise there are several sources of capital.

Seeking Sponsorship: get your act together.
Mel Twelves, *Commercial Officer for Tyne and Wear Museums.*

It is not too many years ago since sponsorship was viewed, particularly in museum circles, as being a less than respectable method of achieving project funding. However, things have now changed to the extent that each year companies receive countless pleas for financial assistance for a variety of projects ranging from local causes to schemes of national or even international interest.

With this increased appetite for sponsorship support, the business has become so competitive that only those organisations that can demonstrate they have a package to offer and can deliver the goods will be able to claim repeated success. Many are, of course, absolute experts in attracting sponsorship but there are others who have not even started to put their act together. Proposals are often ill-prepared, lack planning, promote unrealistic projects, take no account of timing or lack consideration for a sponsor's likely needs. If an applicant is going to have any chance of influencing the management of a potential sponsoring company then such points need to be fully considered before going even so far as to knock on the company's door.

To begin with it must be fully understood that business sponsorship is NOT a form of charitable donation. It is a business expense and as such must clearly show that the business of the sponsor has benefited in some positive way such as promotion of the business name, products or services. This is essential for unless this requirement is met the Inland Revenue will not allow the payment as a deductible expense in computing business profits for tax purposes. (For further explanation a booklet, Business Sponsorship of the Arts – A Tax Guide, by Arthur Andersen & Co. and published by the Association for Business Sponsorship of the Arts is highly recommended).

Before launching a sponsorship raising programme the possibility of obtaining finance through other sources should be fully explored, each project in terms of its practicality and its package assembly. By practicality I refer to the availability of equipment, manpower, co-ordinating competence and time to see the project through. Then there are the packaging questions. Project organisers must be quite clear about the deal they are offering and how far they are prepared to go towards meeting specific sponsorship conditions. A small acknowledgement on a poster or in an exhibition catalogue might satisfy some sponsors but others could be looking for a bit more of the action. I am not suggesting that sponsors should be allowed to dictate or dominate terms and conditions but it is no good meeting a potential sponsor without having a clear policy on some of the more basic points. For example, how and where is the sponsor to be acknowledged? Who is going to handle the promotion and publicity? Should press releases be cleared by both parties? Is sponsorship required in instalments? Who owns title to an event name and to what degree can the sponsor use it to promote products or services? Each project may create its own special terms and conditions but applicants must recognise that involvement of a sponsor could put their own principles under pressure.

If a project has survived the internal analysis stage then the organisers will be faced with the question of who to approach and how and when. It may help to first try and relate the event theme to a specific product type, industry or consumer class (the market). For example for an exhibition of nineteenth century glassware it could be worth looking at some companies currently producing glass products or supplying capital equipment to the glassmaking industry or who themselves are actual consumers of glass. If this fails to produce potential sponsors then an inspection of trade magazines, Sunday supplements, newspapers and various other periodicals might identify those that are particularly active in advertising or seeking to develop their share of the market segment. This knowledge could possibly be turned to advantage. Another option is to try to keep track of at least some of the major companies who have a record of giving sponsorship support. Having gathered this information an afternoon spent looking through the trade directories at the local library can provide worthwhile information on the selected companies. It is often surprising to find out who owns who and the diversity of product and market interest that a company might have. This background information can be very valuable if one gets as far as meeting company management.

Valuable though this information is it can be frittered away if little thought is given to the handling of the initial contact with the company. The very least that should be done is to make a telephone call to establish a company's sponsorship policy and introduce yourself to the right person. The operational structures of companies differ; in some sponsorship is handled by Corporate Affairs whilst in others the right *person could be working in Public Relations, Marketing, Sales or Advertising. An initial telephone contact with the* right *person could be of tremendous value as it might provide a brief introduction to a company's marketing and sponsorship strategies and guide the composition of any subsequent written proposal. It is in the preparation of written proposals that consider-able care needs to be taken. Those that are too long and overbur-dened with reams of supportive literature could very well end up in the waste-bin without being given full consideration. Conversely, if too short and lacking in useful information they may fail to create interest and simply follow the others into the bin. Getting the right balance is not necessarily easy for it is always difficult to resist putting in a few extra 'selling points'. I suggest that the initial proposal should be kept to about one full side of A4 paper but include a brief but realistic outline of a project, an indication of the level of sponsorship required, a few possible benefits to the sponsor and perhaps some background details about the organisation/institution and if appropriate, names of some of its past sponsors. If a company is interested there will be plenty of opportunity to supply more comprehensive information later.*

To the uninitiated the most logical time to submit an application for sponsorship might appear to be when company budgets are in the planning stages. Unfortunately life is not as simple as this. It is true that some companies do encourage applications at such a time but I have found others that claim they do not consider any applications until their budget allocations have been established. And there are those which encourage applications all year round and others who have a selection procedure that demands applications to be sub-mitted at least two years ahead of the project date. To add further confusion there are companies who adopt policies that, for a nomin-ated period of time, limit their sponsorship support to specific types of events whilst others, year in year out, flit from one type of project to another. I recall that in 1984 I noted from the press a particular company had just sponsored an art exhibition and had expressed a desire to be associated with art events. A few months later, full of hope, I contacted the very same company to offer an art project only to be told that art was 'in for this year but next year it was likely to be horse racing'. Frankly the best advice I can give on when to approach is to plan projects well in advance and become acquainted with the procedures of the companies you intend to contact.

There may be many who disagree with my views and approach to sponsorship. They will have had their own successes to support their beliefs and that's the way it should be, for as I have already stated there is no magic formula or recipe that will guarantee success. Applicants must play upon their own strengths; some will have the advantage of a national or international reputation, others an emotive cause. I wish them all the best of luck. My own tactics have been developed because I believe that they improve my chances of success but I will admit to receiving many more refusals than offers. But whatever the opinion I hope that anyone who adopts some of these guidelines will at least receive acknowledgement for having a level of professional input and opportunity for future consideration.

Stock Control and Security

Combining stock keeping and security in one section may seem surprising. In fact the two problems are intertwined. Shop-lifting, and trying to prevent it, may seem a more glamorous subject than how to keep usable stock records, but in terms of profit there is little doubt that more is lost through bad stock-keeping than shop-lifting, and indeed it is in situations where stock-keeping is lax that thefts go undetected.

Whatever your trading, whether it is 6 postcards sold by a museum attendant at the entrance desk cum cloakroom, or a full-blown shop of 5,000 square feet, you are likely to suffer stock losses. These may be from theft, damage or delivery shortfalls.

The best way to minimise losses is by careful housekeeping. You need adequate stock control procedures, so you can identify stock losses quickly. You need to think about your shop layout, not just in terms of convenience to the staff and appeal to the customer, but also in terms of preventing theft. A well-run, well-organised shop, with the staff alert and committed, will suffer fewer of all types of stock loss than a sloppily run operation, where no-one knows what stock they have, no-one feels any sense of commitment to the organisation, or is bothered enough to check deliveries or be alert to shop lifters.

Keeping a stock record

Firstly, you must keep some kind of stock record, so you know what stock you have and what you have sold. Stock control is not a vexatious activity devised by the District Auditor. It is absolutely essential that you know what stock you have, and where it is. It is such a fundamental principle that one would assume its wide acceptance, in both theory and practice. In fact, few museum shops keep

99

accurate stock records – some could not even hazard a guess as to what stock they hold, nor could they locate it easily. Others are so obsessed by fears of stock losses that they impede sales through refusing to keep the stock on open display, and devote more staff time to counting the stock than selling it.

You need to know what stock you have so you can tell what you have sold and can re-order in good time. Through your stock levels you can identify fast, and slow, selling lines, and make judgements on what goods to sell. Only by knowing what stock you have can you work out your likely cash-flow, and avoid or be prepared for any problems. Only by knowing what your stock is, and what you have sold, can you isolate 'shrinkage' through theft or damage.

As a matter of good housekeeping you should stock-take at least once a year (apart from anything else the auditor will demand it). Have your stock-take when stocks are at their lowest. Knowing that the stock-take will happen make sure you ask suppliers for deliveries after, not before or during, stock take. The purpose of the stock-take is to tell you what stock you are holding, both in the warehouse or store and in the shop. All movements of stock betweeen store and shop should be suspended during stock-taking. Stock-taking is also the opportunity to tidy the place up and make sure any one item is stored in one place, rather than several, as this will make subsequent stock control easier.

To carry out the stock-taking, have plenty of stock forms, on which to list the stock. One person should physically count the stock of a specific item, write it on the stock form, then go on to the next item. It is quite likely through the day that odd boxes of goods will be found around the place, and these should be moved back into place, and added to the stock list. It is sensible to number the boxes of each item, and stack them in sequence – this gives a quick visual record of what stock you are holding. Thus, if you have 10,000 cards packed in 6 boxes, label the boxes 1–6, and mark the numbers of cards in each, along with the design. If you label your boxes or packs clearly, it will avoid the problem of staff opening boxes to see what is in them. (It is difficult to control stock once several boxes of the same item are open – stock spills out and is damaged, it is easier to pilfer from because it is hard to detect, and it is hard to know what stock you have if it is made up of half-filled boxes.) Stack the boxes or packs in sequence, with no.1 at the bottom, or stored so that it will be the last to be removed. Then at a glance you can see how many boxes of an item you have, because the one nearest the top, or front is, say box 5, with contents of a gross per box.

Once you have listed the stock, and scrambled it into some kind of order, a second physical count should be made by a 'checker'. Ideally, to avoid collusion, the checker should be an independent person. (You may use a volunteer.) Once the 'checker' has verified the stock list as correct it can then be used as a basis for a variety of action. Firstly, it enables you to do a stock reconciliation. This is like a bank reconciliation, where by checking the transactions, you make sure that what you have in the bank tallies with what your books tell you you have in the bank. With your stock reconciliation you can see if your actual stock is the same as you should have. Take opening stock, add to it new purchases and then deduct stock sold. If you end up with an exact tally, which reconciles, you must be the most unusual retailer in the country. To have no stock loss is virtually impossible, because inevitably some stock will be damaged. Hopefully, if it is received in a damaged condition your staff are well organised enough to return it as faulty to the supplier. If, as is not uncommon, you do not inspect a full consignment, you will without doubt be faced with damaged stock discovered too late for it to be returned. It is up to you to decide if it is worth paying staff to examine goods on delivery, or whether the cost of staff time is unlikely to reveal discrepancies sufficiently great to cover the cost. Ideally, one would, of course, check all deliveries, even to counting bookmarks, but it is quite unrealistic to expect to do so with paid staff.

Apart from goods damaged in transit, and returned to the supplier, you are likely to have stock damaged either through faulty storing or over-handling by customers. You will also have customers returning goods as faulty, or perhaps wanting to exchange items, and the original purchase is somewhat dog-eared, but to secure goodwill you agree. This leaves you with unsaleable goods, which can be used for display purposes, but have to be written off as stock losses. You should make a note of all stock losses through damage, and this will help account for the discrepancies in the stock reconciliation. It will also enable you to decide whether these losses are sufficient to make you want to do something to reduce them (like installing proper racking in a stock room, or telling the staff to be more careful, or putting stock behind glass). You will also be able, when pricing the goods to take into account likely stock losses.

Once you have taken into account loss through damage, you will

101

probably still have shortfalls. These are due to either error – your staff have counted incorrectly, given the wrong amount of change, priced goods incorrectly – or theft, by staff or customers. The stock shortfall that your stock-take reveals will be either too small for you to worry about, or galvanise you into action. Everyone has different standards as to what is an acceptable level of stock loss. There are no hard and fast rules. The figure of 2% is much bandied around in the retail trade as the acceptable level of loss due to theft, and has assumed magical properties and many people will feel perfectly content if their shortfalls from theft are at or below this figure. When planning it seems sensible to allow for total stock losses of around 5%, to be on the safe side. I think one should tolerate stock losses only when to curtail them would in fact reduce sales beyond the saving, and so not be cost effective. Hopefully, by tightening up all procedure up to this point, you will contain stock losses at a level *below* 2% for theft, and 5% overall.

If you are worried about certain items, which seem to be disappearing, as opposed to being sold, then stock-take that item more frequently. Keep your store room in good order, or else much time will be wasted counting and sorting that which has already been counted. If you follow the principle of numbering all boxes it should be possible to save a great deal of duplication of effort. If your stock is not kept in an orderly fashion you will not realise that you still have certain items, and so will not replenish the shop, and will thus miss sales, or re-order when half the old order is still unsold. It helps to mark on the boxes the level at which stock should be re-ordered. This will vary with each item, and will not be necessary for slow selling stock, but for the more popular, fast-selling lines you need to allow yourself enough time to re-order whilst you have stock in hand. Do not wait till you have sold out, because that means lost sales.

You may know what you have ordered, and what stock you have, and have to assume that the difference between the two is stock that has been sold. If you are just taking cash for sales, and counting up the total at the end of the day, without attempting any break-down, either by coding on the till or keeping a manual sales sheet you are, in a sense, guessing when there are shortfalls as to what exactly has been paid for and what is apparently missing. For example, your takings for the day are £800. You may have stock tickets for some of the more expensive items or books, but are you going to record every postcard sale, by design? It is not actually practicable.

You can keep records of what you sell either by coding each item, and keying it in on the till for each transaction, or by making a note on a pre-printed (or duplicated) stock sheet. In future you will be able to use light pens to read off the codes on each purchase (but these types of tills are too expensive and unreliable at present). The problems of keeping sales records at point of sale are that it is hard to maintain the system if you are under pressure, because it takes time, and the clamour of people trying to get served before they rejoin their coach means you need an iron will to take time to record each purchase. Also, generally people will make mistakes when keeping the records, by pressing the wrong till buttons or ticking the wrong column. It is advisable to back up any record keeping at the till, with a physical check of stock in the shop (either daily or weekly). The real problem with these types of checks is that they are easy to do in quiet times and hard on busy days, when turnover is high, yet it is after the busy days that you need the checks, for re-ordering, and to pick up thefts.

By tabbing your products, for example, asking the printer to pack cards in 50's or 100's you can try to make a rough and ready check on sales as you go along, without a precise count. You might find it helpful to work out the retail value of each box in your store, so if you are selling 2 boxes of item A (with a retail value of £100 per box) and 4 boxes of item B (with a retail value of £60 a box), you can make a rough correlation with cash received.

If the boxes are going down quickly, but the takings remain low, it should sound an alarm bell in your mind. Of course, if you never visit the stock room, you cannot make this kind of check, and your stock may be spirited away and sold on street markets up and down the land without your realising it. (This is, of course, in the unlikely event of your stock being saleable in any market in the country!)

You must make your stock secure wherever it is stored. Keep your stock room locked, and keep the key safely, limit the number of people authorised to visit the stock room. The presence of any un-authorised person, or any unnecessary visit should arouse suspicion. If you cannot have a stock room, and are storing items in cupboards, or under the counters, you should still make an effort to protect them. Your budget may not stretch to purpose built cupboards, or metal cages on wheels, but consider such makeshift devices as tying the boxes together with string (or chains?) so that any thief would hopefully be deterred by the time it took to disentangle a box. Of course it is not practicable to construct an Emmett-like security system, but a measure of common sense will go 90% of the way to protecting your stock.

Theft

60% of all losses through theft are estimated to be the result of staff stealing from their employers. The dreaded shoplifter is thought to account for 25% (although in department stores detectives put this figure higher at 30–35%). The other 15% of losses through theft are attributed to burglaries and break-ins.

Very few museum shops are likely to suffer a burglary. The building is generally too secure after closing time, and the museum shops stock simply not attractive nor valuable enough to attract either the professional or the casual thief. Burglary is possible and one should take the usual general sensible precautions to make it difficult for the burglar to gain entrance, and once inside to get to the stock. Do not leave money in an accessible place (like the till, or a drawer under the counter). Leave the till drawer open at night, so a thief does not force it open.

Those responsible for running museum shops worry disproportionately about shoplifters. They should worry more about staff theft – after all, your staff can steal from you every day, whereas the shoplifter is an occasional visitor. Theft by staff arises because they see the management of the shop as slapdash, and this encourages those dishonestly inclined, to feel there is little risk of being caught. Without this deterrent they can devise more and more sophisticated ways of stealings. The best way of preventing theft by staff is to keep an orderly operation. It should be apparent to customers and staff alike that any thefts will be quickly noticed. This is only possible if you keep your stock in some kind of order, and are seen to stock take. Similarly, make sure that staff, whether in the warehouse store or shop are liable to unexpected visits by senior management. (If you have only one person running the shop, then the museum curator, accountant, head porter, whoever, should be encouraged to drop in to the shop unannounced). If people are likely to be interrupted they cannot risk being caught in the act. If you never visit the stock room, and you only go to the shop at 2 o'clock every day, it makes life easier for the thief.

Visiting and being visible are the most important factors in deterring one particular type of staff theft, which is, in fact, unusual, but not unknown in museum shops and this is collusion by warehouseman and supplier, to sign for deliveries not in fact received. This type of fraud, which can be very costly to say a supermarket chain, or department store, is less likely in a museum store because of the relatively low volume of goods, and its specific nature. Some museum shops are so lax about keeping records of their ordering that an unscrupulous supplier could supply and invoice for goods not ordered, and if the museum shop is chaotic enough the supplier could even invoice and not bother to deliver the goods, and still expect the invoice to be paid!

It is very usual for staff in a museum shop to help themselves to the odd postcard, just as office staff take home stationery and use the office photocopier to run off leaflets for the scouts jumble sale. Try to teach the staff that stock costs money, and that any stock losses eat into profits. Offer a discount to staff on their purchases, because this makes clear to them that they are expected to pay for goods, not to take them. If the staff are interested in the museum's specialist fields, they may be tempted to steal books. Encourage them to read the display copy – let them borrow it, with permission, when the shop is closed.

More costly than staff theft of stock is theft of money from the till. Money is more attractive as an object of theft than goods, so you have to be particularly diligent in guarding it. Keep all the money in a till, or a safe. Do not allow the till to be used as a petty cash box. If you do, it means that anyone seen taking money from the till can claim to be taking it out for a purpose.

All sales should be rung up on the till, because then you have a record of all monies taken. A usual fraud is for staff not to ring up all sales, and to put the cash in a separate drawer of the till. For example, the sale is for £5, the till opened on a 'void' or 'no sale' button and the £5 put in a back compartment. At the end of the day the fraudulent cashier pockets the surplus cash. If challenged they may claim it is the float, or deny all knowledge of the money. So be suspicious of the till being opened when no sale is recorded. (The till roll at the end of the day will show the incidence of 'voids'). Ask your staff to put notes in the till for every occasion on which the till is opened without money being put in. It is easiest to have a pad by the till for this purpose. The valid reasons will be for example, incorrect change given; asked to give change; cash taken out to bank; cash taken out to get more change.

Another fraud is the false purchase trick. This is a fraud against the customer rather than the employer, but it is no more tolerable for that. This is a fraud used in supermarkets. It probably will not be used in museum shops, though could be. The cashier keeps an item by the till – say a guide book. When ringing up the purchases she adds on the cost of the guide book. It is not given to the customer, but is there in case the customer queries the bill, in which case the cashier asks, 'Is the guide book not yours?' It will be passed off as an understandable error. The cashier merely has to note how many of these purchases have been over-charged, and put notes in the till saying 'over-rang'. The clever fraud will vary the amounts. Detection is more likely if the thief gets too greedy, and the number of over-rings arouses suspicion.

A more usual fraud by a cashier is to under-ring the amount due. The customer's money is taken, say for £5 worth of purchases, but only £4 rung up on the till. For the fraud to work the customer must not notice the discrepancy on the till, and that is why retailers like tills that give receipts and totals. (The cheapest tills do not give receipts, just keep one total on the till roll). The cashier should be told to ring up on the till before taking money, so the customer has a chance to see the total. (The customer becomes the retailer's supervisor). One famous store owner used to say a receipt on the floor is money in the drawer – which means that though the customer may throw away the receipt, the possibility of the customer checking that the amount he paid tallies with the amount shown on the receipt acts as a deterrent.

A similar fraud to under-ringing, i.e. not recording sales and putting the money in a separate part of the till, is to simply by-pass the till, and neither ring up sales nor put the money in the till, but to pocket it. This fraud is quite risky because there is a good chance of someone seeing the money being pocketed.

Modern tills have the ability to give a printout and total of all sales for the day by pressing what is usually known as the 'Z' key. To stop a dishonest cashier from cashing up at say 4 o'clock and then planning to steal the takings recorded between 4 and 5 o'clock by destroying the 'Z' record produced by the till for that period, the till will number consecutively each 'Z' record, and you should check you have them all. (To lose a 'Z' record is like losing a cheque from the cheque book; you certainly would not tolerate missing cheques, so be similarly careful about missing till receipts).

All types of theft from the till can be deterred by making it quite clear that detection is likely. What you are looking for are patterns of behaviour that seem suspicious. For example, if you have different staff on the till do takings drop regularly when one person is on the till. Are there reasons for this – for example, half day closing or market day – is that staff member simply horrid and unhelpful to customers, or is there something more suspicious behind it. Are there an awful lot of notes about over-rings when one person is on the till – perhaps they are simply incompetent, or is it a clue to theft? Usually a sharp eye will pick up theft. You can institute test purchasing – this is what happens in department stores, on a regular basis. A person will be asked to make purchases, of quite a lot of items, and later you can see from the till roll whether the correct amount has been rung up. Of course, you would need to make quite a number of test purchases before you are likely to uncover fraud, even where it is going on.

If your staff are going to steal from you in a very sophisticated way – for example, by tampering with the computer records so that the stock figures support sales figures, they give themselves time, but ultimately should be discovered by the old fashioned physical stock check and bank reconciliation. Do not be rushed into believing that all fraud is not capable of detection. 90% of would-be thieves will be deterred by the risk of detection when your efficient stock system makes it likely. Of the remaining 10%, 9% are too stupid to recognise that they are likely to be caught by vigilant supervision. Perhaps 1% can expect to go undetected for any length of time – and if your stock control system is good then the time should be limited – and hopefully you will have caught them before they move on. (Be careful always to check references – including the last employer – sometimes the person may have been asked to leave and prosecution waived. You need to know that).

Shoplifting

You can vet your staff, but you cannot vet each customer, and ask if they had previous convictions for shoplifting, nor should you treat all potential customers as criminals. Putting up signs of the 'shop-lifters will be prosecuted' type and running the shop as a fortress, with all stock under guard, will not only deter customers, it may put the idea of stealing into their heads. At one London Transport station new lifts were installed, which the manufacturer advertised as vandal-proof – what a challenge! Similarly, do not suggest to customers that stealing is usual behaviour for visitors to your shop. In America the trust system is widely used in museums and museum stores, and this implication of expected standards of behaviour seems to have effect. When the Smithsonian Institute decided for all its museum shops to increase customer access to goods, shoplifting did not increase as a percentage of turnover. (It increased, but sales increased at a faster rate which meant an overall increase in profits).

Shoplifters in museum shops seem to fall into two main categories – the book thief and school parties. The book thief is often a very persistent, repeated offender. Books seem especially vulnerable, and seem to attract a double-standard for a certain kind of thief, who somehow feels justified in stealing books (as if charging for them were a tax on learning, against which he is demonstrating). To catch a book thief, as any shoplifter, there are some cardinal rules. Firstly, make sure your shop does not have blind corners, you should be able to observe clearly all parts of the shop, and all customers in it. You may need mirrors to ensure this is possible, or even consider re-organising the shop. Do not have display islands for customers to hide behind. Be suspicious of customers who do not behave as the usual customer, for example if they seem more interested in you and their surroundings, rather than the stock. Most shoplifters take time to achieve their object, so approach all customers enquiring if you can help, and re-approach browsers. This apparent attentiveness will deter all but the most determined shoplifters. Get used to watching customers hands, rather than their faces. Shoplifters use their hands to steal with. Be suspicious of large overcoats or bags, into which items could be slipped. Watch any customer who is moving stock around – for example, picking up a book, looking through it and replacing it at the end of the stand rather than in its correct place. He may be assembling his loot. A very usual technique for the shoplifter to use is to place gloves or hat or newspaper over an item and scoop it up with the gloves etc. That way it may be un-detected, and could possibly be passed off as an accident. Look out for the customer who switches round price tags – relabelling the expensive with the cheaper label – using the labels which come off in three parts makes this harder for a thief.

If you cannot achieve unobscured views of the whole shop then use mirrors; concave give the widest view. It is sensible to use mirror for example on pillars, as part of the decor of the shop; mirrors are great deterrents to shoplifters, because they are uncertain as to whether they can be seen or not, and from which direction.

Shoplifting by children is very difficult to deal with – the best thing is to prevent it. The main problem is that a swarm of children, all clamouring for attention descend on the shop, and there are not enough members of staff to deal with them. Each child seems to have four hands each, all are intent on handling all the stock, before they decide on their purchases and in the mêleé it is easy for children to pocket small items unobserved. Some of the children are predisposed to do so, as they see theft as a display of cunning, approved by their peer group. Do not treat children as potential thieves, by banning them from your shop – they are a valuable source of revenue, and anyway you have a responsibility to make their visit enjoyable, because they are the visitors of the future. Do not put up signs which indicate that you expect children to steal – of the 'children will only be admitted two at a time when supervised by an adult' variety. It may be best to set up a children's corner, or counter, perhaps outside the main shop, where they can swarm round and clamour, without disturbing other customers, or having access to the more valuable stock items. Children do like to finger things, even when there is not the least chance of their buying them, and it may be sensible to limit the potential damage.

Decide ahead of time what you are going to do if you see someone shoplifting. Are you going to make a citizen's arrest and detain the shoplifter whilst awaiting the police? Are you going to prosecute, and lose staff time, because they will be called to give evidence. You may decide that you will prosecute if the level of theft is high, and not for small amounts. Whatever you decide is up to you, but do think about it before the event and discuss it with staff – there is no point in having a policy that the staff are unhappy about enforcing.

Clearly some stock of particular value will need more protection than others. Easily pocketable items, such as rings or brooches, should be kept in a cabinet, but remember that they should be easily visible. There is no point in running a total secure, theft proof shop if it is also a customer-proof shop. It is better to allow in your costings for a certain amount of stock loss, and concentrate your energies on boosting sales. Keep careful stock records, and watch staff rather than shoplifters as the most costly sources of theft.

Summary

To minimise stock losses, keep careful account of your stock. Check deliveries; keep stock in a secure area; stock-take annually. You are more likely to suffer losses through staff than shoplifters. Set up strict procedures, and carry out spot-checks. Make detection likely. To combat shoplifting be vigilant, avoid blind corners, but remember you are running a shop, not a fortress.

Pricing

Fixing the prices at which you sell things depends on:—

1. The cost of the item;
2. The selling price of the same item in other outlets;
3. The price of similar goods in your own and other outlets;
4. The perceived value – will it seem reasonable to the customer.

Do not automatically fix prices by taking cost price, marking up 100% and adding VAT. If you do this, you will end up with the following problems – firstly you will get very odd prices, like 84p or £2.67p. These odd looking prices will stop the customer in his tracks, and make him think about the price at a crucial juncture, when you do not want him to have any second thoughts. Have prices which are usual – for example, 95p or 99p or £1.95 or £1.75. You only have to look round at any shop (even the greengrocers) to see that some prices are more used than others, for example, very few products are priced at 7p or 17p or 27p, or 4p or 14p or 16p and 26p; it is more usual to round up the figures. Manufacturers are usually aware of this and price their products,and recommend selling prices accordingly.

Have prices which make change giving easy. If you are frequently faced by school or coach parties, all clamouring to pay and get back on the bus, anticipate the problem of pricing goods in a way most likely to avoid change giving. Of course, you cannot price postcards at £1 because the postcard purchaser most usually tenders a one pound coin, but you have got control over both how you price your goods and what you stock and the need to have goods that can be easily sold in terms of the trouble they generate at the till should be considered.

This leads logically on to 'price pointing', meaning have items at every price that customers want to pay. Analyse what you are offering in each category (say mineral samples or children's items or replicas) in terms of its selling price. You may, to your surprise, find you have 20 items under £1, 1 item at £1.75 and 4 at £6.95. (This is an extreme example.) You may then think to yourself – do we need 20 items at under £1 – would those customers not still buy if the selection were smaller (and that would make it easier for ordering, for stock control and save space). Could you not then buy more items in the £1–£6 category. You cannot make these decisions in the abstract, they have to relate to what is on offer, but it does help you think about your stock, and potential customers. Actual sales should be analysed in terms of price pointing to see at what prices items are selling best. As with all analysis of figures you have to be sensible when considering them – do not assume that because 20 items below £1 are selling best in volume terms, you would not sell well, and perhaps more profitably, an item at £2.50, a price at which you have nothing to offer. With price pointing you are posing the question 'are we missing sales by not offering goods at certain price levels?' Price is only one factor, you may be missing sales because you are not offering attractive goods, but price should be considered as part of the equation.

Overall, you will probably want to work on a 100% mark-up. (This means you double the cost price and add VAT to fix a selling price.) Books are usually subject to the NET book agreement so have to be sold at the stated cover price, fixed by the publisher, and the mark-up on a book is usually 50% so if you are to achieve your average mark-up of 100% (which is probably the minimum to cover all operating costs, allow for theft, damage, slow selling stock and make a profit) you will have to fix a mark-up higher than 100% on some items to achieve an overall average. You are unlikely to be able to mark-up more than 100% on goods that are generally available in other outlets, because you do not want a reputation for being an expensive place to shop. When selecting items cost and likely selling price are important. Often one finds attractive products that are too expensive – the same customer may buy an item at Harrods they would reject as too expensive in a museum shop. It is not just because of the perceived value of the item, but because the customer in the museum shop is usually not expecting to spend much – the main purpose of the visit was to see the museum, not to go shopping, and so the visitor is not mentally prepared to spend, and impulse buying has quite a lot working against it – the customer does not need the item, so is likely to find reasons for not buying it as well as justifications for so doing, and price can be critical either as a deterrent or an incentive. You want the price to trigger off in the customer the response 'that's good value, I should buy it now while I have the opportunity'.

If you only fix the price by doubling the cost price, you will find that your stock suffers from price inconsistency – that is, that similar goods are different prices. This is foolish as it raises questions in the customers' minds that can all too easily dissuade them from making any purchase at all. Having inconsistent pricing does not mean choice for the customer, it means that you are selling something too cheaply or too expensively because there should be a correct price. For example, postcards should all be one price, unless there are obvious differences – for example, size or you may charge more for postcards from foreign museums. But in both these cases the difference will be clear to the customer.

The cost price of an item and its selling price in other outlets will determine the selling price of many items in your shop. There is much greater flexibility when the products have been commissioned and specifically produced for your museum shop. Then you take into account the cost (including the capital investment) and the perceived value of the product, which put crudely means what you can get away with charging. Hopefully the product will be sufficiently special to command a premium price. Some products, like printed items, can be inexpensively produced in relation to their selling price, and you may be able to charge mark-ups of 500%. Do not feel that this is excessive, it it gives you a selling price which compares well with similar products, or which you judge the market will bear. The 100% mark-up is an overall target, not one of the ten commandments. If you can maintain sales at much higher levels you will increase the profits.

Inflation has been a fairly consistent feature of our society for decades, and it must be remembered when fixing prices. Firstly, when buying goods prices may seem high, but be aware that the prices are future prices for the next year, and that what seems like a high price may just be keeping abreast of inflation. Secondly, and more importantly, re-price your goods to keep in line with the price rises of other items. So if you have 5 years' supply of postcards, do not sell them at the same price for 5 years if the price of postcards has risen during the period. Make sure you adjust your prices, because your money is being tied up in that unsold stock, and the value of the money is being eroded by inflation, and you should try to maintain

113

the value of your stock by repricing. Failure to do so not only means lost profits, it also means you will get price inconsistencies in your stock.

Should you try price reductions to get rid of slow moving stock, or to stimulate interest? It is the norm rather than the exception in American museum shops for there to be a 'special offers' section of discounted items. Sales and price reductions are much rarer in museums shops in the UK. It can, however, be used effectively in certain circumstances. An annual sale is a good way of creating interest, and drawing customers specifically to the museum shop. You must let people know that the sale is happening (by circulating the Friends Association, distributing and displaying handbills and by advertising in the local press – remember editorial coverage is more effective than paid advertising). The best publicity will be word of mouth by satisfied customers. If you are having a sale, then it is best to limit it to a few days, or even one day, rather than letting it drag on. There are some items that will not sell at any price, for example, postcards of slugs. Such items can be mixed in with others – for example, a selection of 25 postcards for £1 – and include in each selection five slugs as well as a few more attractive cards. You could give unsaleable items away as a free gift with every purchase over £5. When you are selling discounted stock, try to pile it high, to give it impact and importance. In a sale you can afford to be more brash than you would normally be – and use the techniques of the mass retailer, rather than the bookseller. Try to make your sale fun, give plenty of bargains. Go to the back of the stock-room, and take the opportunity of the sale to try to shift goods that have been there for decades (they may take on a new antique look!). As well as a sale you may want to have a 'special offer' section. Try to make this eye-catching. Make sure it does not look musty, or it will become a non-selling area. Because of the risk of this it may be better just to have a good clear-out at a sale, rather than a 'special offers' section.

How much do you have to reduce an item before it sells must depend on the item. It has to be a significant amount either by value or percentage to attract attention. Half-price is the best reduction to attract buyers, but your ability to reduce prices by this amount will depend on what you paid for them, and how much you are prepared to lose. Remember that unsold stock is costing you money, at the very least the foregone interest, but more because it could be buying you more stock which would sell, and earn you gross profits of up to

100%, and it is taking up valuable storage space. So be greedy for salvaging your investment, and if you think reducing the price will shift slow selling stock then reduce the price.

Summary

Your prices depend not just on the cost of the item, but also on the price of comparable items in your own and other outlets. Also, an item must seem good value. You must offer goods over a range of prices to satisfy various levels of the market. Price reductions may help sales.

Staff

Whatever the difficulties and drawbacks of your shop (poor position, starved of capital, poor storage facilities) good staff will overcome them, and bad staff will add to them. The staff, the people responsible for the shop and working in it, are the most critical factor in determining the success of your trading. There are shops in the most unpromising situations – in museums with objects which do not translate well into saleable items, where the curator and staff disapprove of trade, and set a damper on morale, where the shop is tucked away at the back of the museum, away from visitors, and where the conditions in the shop are cramped – yet one can find that a committed and enterprising staff have overcome the difficulties and turned the shop into an Aladdin's cave. They have made sure there are signposts throughout the museum to show the shop is there, and managed to mobilise a Friends Group to help in the shop, and find it customers.

Conversely, bad staff not only fail to make the most of what there is, they sit and moan, thus demoralising others, and giving a very unpleasant, unwelcoming feel to the shop and museum. Bad staff have a habit of lowering everybody's standards and morale, so you have to be careful that potentially good staff are not turned into bad staff by bad example.

The most important thing about your shop or trading company staff is that you make each and everyone of them responsible for their actions. Give your head of trading the power to make decisions (working to pre-determined criteria) and then hold him responsible for those decisions. It is very usual when dealing with museum trading to go into very limp, pathetic shops, and have, when questioning staff, to listen to a series of excuses, in which everybody is blamed for the shop's obvious shortcomings, except the staff themselves. ('The shop display is bad because "they" won't give us the money for proper fittings'; 'The cleaners are terrible, and you can't say anything to them'; 'We can't put more stock out because the stock

116

room is so far away'.) All these have been given as excuses. The staff must look at ways of overcoming difficulties and deal with the problems rather than dealing out excuses.

It should be clear when appointing staff that they are going to be held responsible for their actions, and any tendency to blame other people should be treated very quickly and firmly. This is not to say that the correct management style is to march into the shop, bark at staff and refuse to listen to explanations. Hectoring people, however enjoyable to the person doing it, has never been known to produce results. A soft word, along the lines 'isn't this shop horribly dirty, we must clean it up at once' should be all that is needed. Make sure if you have given an instruction that it is obeyed. If you are seen as giving orders, but never seeing that they are carried out, you cannot then believe that in giving the orders in the first place you have done your job. You are telling people to do something because it needs doing, if they do not do it the need remains. If the staff ignore your instructions because they think your decision is wrong they may feel they are justified – but this is not so – if they want to question your instruction that is perfectly acceptable – there is a great deal of evidence that authoritarian management produces poor results – but they must be prepared to tell you that they are not going to carry out orders, not leave you to discover the task is not done. You are employing grown-ups and want them to act in a grown-up way. By treating the staff as grown-ups, responsible and capable, you should get the desired results. If you give your staff responsibility and make it clear that they are responsible, you will hopefully get into the position that they will not blame other people, or be unjustly blamed themselves, and they will take pride in the work which is known to be theirs (and be praised for it). When writing about responsibility one seems to be emphasising attributing blame. In face, making people responsible for their work in understood parameters, gives more opportunity for pleasure and job satisfaction.

Choosing staff

If the museum has its own trading company then the directors of the company will generally choose the manager. If there is no member or representative of the curatorial staff on the Board then it may be prudent to invite one on to the interviewing panel. Once the senior appointment has been made (indeed, there may only be one member of staff) when making subsequent appointments the manager of the trading company should be allowed to make his own selection, perhaps with the help of one or two board members if it is a senior enough appointment to warrant it. It is not right to have the Board select staff for the manager, nor, as was the practice in one museum, to allow retiring museum wardens the automatic right to supplement their pensions by becoming sales staff in the museum shop! When you think about staff and staff recruitment you would not begin to think that such things could happen, but it is extraordinary how often in museum trading these indefensible recruitment practices occur.

When recruiting staff what should you look for? To some extent this depends on temperament. What type of person will fit in with your existing staff (or be sufficiently forceful not to be depressed by them!). If your museum style is academic and scholarly, and that is how you want it, then you will not be happy with a brash entrepreneur who wishes to have a shop that looks like a cross between Tesco and a souvenir shop. You need someone who likes the museum and what it represents, and who respects its values. A fanatical interest in the museum's area of interest is not necessary – indeed it might be undesirable as it can lead to contempt of those who are less knowledgeable and a refusal to stock popular items that are not authentic or sufficiently accurate to satisfy the purist. There is a great deal of difference between indifference and fanaticism, and you want staff who will take a intelligent interest in the museum's collection. You may find that a university graduate fits in better with the curatorial staff.

You do not necessarily need someone with previous publishing or commercial experience. The problem with experienced staff is that they may have learnt bad habits. A sensible, intelligent person who has an enquiring mind, and learns from their mistakes is more value than any previous experience. Previous experience is only of value if the person is intelligent enough to learn from that experience, rather than slavishly imitating it. Knowing how other organisations organise similar operations does not mean that you know the best way. Be particularly cautious of certain types of previous experience – publishers are notoriously unbusinesslike, and you may in fact be demanding a more commercial approach, whereas people coming

118

from publishing may expect a museum to be less concerned with making money.

Staff management and training

Make clear to all your staff, when selecting them for the job, and consistently during their employment, what you want the organisation to be like, what you want it to achieve and how you want that done. You cannot get what you want by making people guess what it is. To let the staff know you have to know yourself – and often, in fact usually, neither those responsible for the museum nor those responsible for the shop have thought through exactly what they expect the museum's trading to do.

Assuming you have told the staff (and everyone else concerned with the shop) what you hope it will achieve, keep them informed as to how well the criteria are being met. If your aim is profit tell the staff if you are making as much profit as your target, more than the same period last year, less than forecast. Tell them if you have had compliments or complaints about stock, service, display. Keep them informed (it encourages them, it makes them feel responsible, it increases job satisfaction and it eliminates demoralising rumours).

Some organisations hold regular weekly staff meetings, where all the staff discuss the plan of work for the week, and apportion responsibility for the individual tasks. In theory such meetings mean the staff are all kept informed, feel involved in the work and work well, in an open, democratic manner. In practice such meetings can deteriorate into back-biting, and navel-gazing (where everyone is preoccupied with fundamental questioning of their purpose and prefer the consideration of problems to the resolution of them). Any staff meeting has to be well managed, with clearly defined purpose. It must not degenerate into back-biting. It must not be a time-wasting exercise, used to put off doing disagreeable jobs – it is usually pleasanter to sit around chatting than to restock, count change, or dust shelves.

Even if your staff are capable, interested and lively when they join you, they will get stale if they stay in the shop. Send them to look at

119

other museum shops (and ask them to write a brief report on their findings, highlighting good points which you could adopt and bad points to avoid). Send them to look at up-market gift shops (for example in Covent Garden) where they will find a concentration of new ideas that may be ahead of their time, but could be pointers to gift ideas of the future.

Encourage them to look at your own museum's collection, and familiarise themselves with items on display – so they will feel able to deal with customers' enquiries from an informed standpoint. Let the shop staff visit the museum during working hours, rather than expecting them to visit on their day off. Let them go and view any new exhibitions or displays – encourage them to complete (unaided) any trail sheets put out by the museum (so they are in a position to recommend it to customers). Do not let staff absent themselves from the shop without permission on the pretext that they are visiting the museum and in so doing are carrying out your instructions.

Take advantage of the courses organised by MUSPUB (the Group for Museum Publishing and Shop Management) and AIM (the Association of Independent Museums). Both provide opportunities to meet people working in the field, as well as the formal content of their seminars and conferences. You may even want to send staff to the American Museum Stores Association Annual Convention, at which there are literally dozens of lectures and workshops, all on the subject of museum trading. If sending staff to courses discourage them from going in twos and just talking to each other; make clear to them that they are the representatives of your museum and must conduct themselves in a responsible and responsive manner. Encourage them to report back on what they have learnt – and something beyond 'Oh, they didn't say anything new'. Send them with a specific brief – you may even want to be formal enough to have a check list for staff to complete after going to conferences, along the lines:

'Name of conference, organised by, date, location; speakers (attach programme if available), other delegates (attach list if available). Points raised useful to this museum. New ideas we could use – and difficulties to watch for. Useful information to compare our performance against.'

If you keep such information filed together, it can be useful not only for new staff, but also to maintain a list of contacts. For example, if you are producing a new publication and want to sell it to a museum with a similar collection you might be able to personalise the approach by looking up the name of the relevant person from delegates lists. (It might be easier to phone the museum and ask the name of the relevant person, but having been to the same conference you could try to strike a more familiar and friendly note along the lines of 'You may not remember me but . . .' or 'You met a colleague of mine at . . .'. When asking for favours it certainly helps.

Not all your staff will be good at all the jobs that need to be done. The skill of good management here as anywhere else is to recognise the strengths and weaknesses of individuals, and try to make the most and least of them respectively. (Industrial psychologists teach as their first rule 'You can't change anyone's behaviour, only they can change themselves'.) You are unlikely to persuade staff to change bad habits over-night. They may change over a period of time, if you can motivate them to do so, but some shortcomings you must simply be aware of, and act to counteract. For example, if one member of staff is full of enthusiasm but hopeless at keeping the paperwork in order, try to devise a system to deal with that. Some faults, such as fear of using initiative or taking decisions, are due to lack of confidence, and may recede as good experience and praise build confidence. In many instances it is not simply that a particular member of staff has particular defects but rather that they are not equally good at all aspects of the job. Try to recognise which things particular staff are good at and try to dovetail the skills of the whole staff so they can work well as a team.

There are some basic techniques in salesmanship that are taught fairly routinely in the induction courses of large-scale retailers. Staff must be neatly dressed and well-groomed; their speech must be at the right volume; their personality friendly, courteous, tactful and patient. Sales staff must advance towards the customer and create involvement with them. Interest the customer in the merchandise (on which the sales staff must be knowledgeable, but not opinionated). Listen to the customer and ask questions, encourage the customer to handle the merchandise. Offer the customer another item of merchandise which would complement the purchase. If you strike up a relationship with the customer it makes it harder for them to walk out without buying anything.

Some staff are irredeemably bad. At best they are unsuited to the job, at worst they are unfit for any job! Do not keep bad staff once you are sure that they cannot be improved. If you are unhappy about their performance then it is unlikely that they are getting much pleasure out of the job either. Do not be careless about people's lives and welfare – hiring and firing people is very serious, but if you are sure that someone is in the wrong job your responsibility to your museum and them is to tell them, and try to work out a plan for their leaving. Tell them frankly that they are in the wrong job, that the job is not making the most of their talents, and that they should look for alternative employment. Depending on the circumstances, and remember it is your fault for choosing them in the first place, give them as long as 6 months to look for another job. It is surprising how responsible people are when treated responsibly. They do not mess around during this very extended period of notice, and if they do you can always ask them to leave more quickly. Generally they appreciate that there is a problem, and if you have handled it well they will not feel a loss of confidence, but rather that their potential is not being used, and that they will do better and be happier elsewhere. They should appreciate your solicitude. If you are not working with people in a friendly, caring atmosphere, all this may seem like pie in the sky and you are likely to find yourself brought in front of an industrial tribunal. There are very clear guidelines on employment rights available from the Department of Employment. Familiarise yourself with them. Staff who are dishonest, or slovenly and lack any commitment to the work will, of course, need firmer, more abrasive handling. Be fair, keep other staff informed (but do not discuss people's personal affairs) to minimise the anxiety that staff changes cause, and be accessible to people. Do not hide behind the excuse of the trade unions for failing to deal with the problem of unsuitable staff. If the union or staff association has involvement in staff appointments take the trouble to keep them informed of your actions. Take the attitude and tone that the unions share with you the wish to make the shop profitable – since that is the way to preserve jobs.

Keep your staff informed, involve them in decision making and try to keep them lively. However good your team do not be misled into believing that you must preserve the team at all cost. You need new blood, and should welcome a fresh infusion from time to time. (One of the ways management consultants measure the good health of a company is by 'age profile' – are the staff old, and growing older, or are new young staff being recruited). Looking for new jobs is not a betrayal – if the staff are not ambitious for themselves they will not be ambitious for your shop.

As well as your regular staff there are periods of the year, or week, or day in which you are particularly busy. Rather than have staff under employed in the quiet times, think of recruiting part-time or temporary staff. The local Job Centre may operate a register for temporary employment and you will usually be able to find students or new graduates wanting a short term job. Ask the Job Centre what the going rate for the job is – if it is more than you are prepared to offer stick to your guns – a job in a museum is much more pleasant and interesting than most alternatives. The only time to pay more is if you are desperate and cannot get anyone to work for the money you are offering. You have to calculate when employing staff not just whether you need more people to get through the work, but rather are the additional members of staff generating enough extra trade to cover their costs, and hopefully a bit more!

Volunteers

As well as paid staff you may consider using volunteers. The often mooted fear of trouble with the unions if introducing volunteers is unlikely to arise if you are firstly working in consultation with them, and secondly not replacing any paid jobs. A great many museum shops, especially in the USA and Canada, depend heavily on volunteers for staffing. The first thing that should be said about voluntary workers is that they must know that the emphasis is on 'work' not 'voluntary'. Volunteers are seeking, most generally, companionship, interest and a sense of helping a worthwhile cause, and the job satisfaction that an employee expects. To keep your volunteers happy you have to show them that what they are doing is important. You cannot thank them often enough. Try to make occasions on which volunteers can meet each other (building up the social side) for example, invite them to the private view of special exhibitions, starting with a glass of sherry in the shop. If you have enough volunteers, organise an annual outing, to another museum, or stately home. Realise that your volunteers become very devoted supporters, and often your best customers!

How do you find volunteers? The first thing is a notice asking for volunteers in the entrance hall of the museum or at the information desk. Approach the Volunteer Bureau of your local Council of

Voluntary Service, and ask them to circulate enquirers with your vacancies. Ask large-scale employers in your area to circulate their pensioners with your request (this can produce a very good response). The local newspaper may have a social service column, through which it appeal for voluntary workers. The best source once you are established is word of mouth.

It is important to make clear to your volunteers exactly what you want them to do. Give them clearly defined responsibilities. Because they are not being paid does not mean they can be sloppy. You must impose on volunteers the standards you require of paid staff. Usually this is to the volunteers' liking, as it makes them feel their work is important – if you have volunteers who will not do the work that needs doing ('I hate going to the stock room'; 'I don't do the hoovering at home so I'm not doing it here') or comport themselves in an unseemly fashion, thus damaging the image of the shop, you must get rid of them. The best way of doing this is consistently giving them unpleasant jobs, out of the public's gaze. They will probably leave – with no hard feelings towards the museum – and make sure to thank them fulsomely.

Whether volunteers or paid staff, the people running your shop are the most important asset, or liability, you have. Good staff are invaluable, but not irreplaceable. Your organisation should be such that you make the best of what talents your staff have, and provide the cheerful, supportive atmosphere in which they are likely to excel. Neither adopt, not tolerate, the attitude 'It will do'; that is an acceptance of a minimum standard. Learn constantly – that way at least costly mistakes become valuable lessons. If you do not have a fresh, inquisitive attitude towards your job you will be bored by it, and this will show. Keep it fun for you, all the staff, and the customers. Remember, that for many visitors the only contact they will have with museum staff is with the sales attendants in the shop.

Summary

Good staff are critical to the success of any trading. Let staff know what is expected of them. Give responsibility. Encourage outside contacts. However good your team, you need fresh blood. Recruit temporary staff for busy periods. Consider using volunteers, and apply the same high standards to them.

Reaching a market beyond the museum

Once you are producing goods for your museum shop it is very tempting to try to extend your market beyond the physical confines of your museum shop. This section examines some of the possible ways this can be done, and includes contributions from people who have specific experience.

Wholesaling

Museums originating their own products to sell in their own shop, may be well advised to wholesale them. That is sell the items to other outlets for re-sale. The main advantages of selling to other outlets are that it increases the museum's ability to produce its own products, by lessening the amount of capital it needs to tie up in the product (because the rate of sales is speeded up by adding the sales to other retailers to the sales through the shops). If you are able to increase your stock turn on own products, you will have the capital to initiate more. The museum trading company can increase the production run, and this should reduce unit costs (because the origination can be amortised over larger quantities). Products clearly identified as having been originated by your museum publicise your museum to a wider audience, hopefully stimulating interest in the museum itself, and encouraging visitors. If your goods are of good quality, it will improve the image of your museum to a wider audience, who will value the museum's continued existence. Even though you are selling goods wholesale at a lower price than you get as a retailer, your wholesaling operation should still be profitable, and increase your profits overall.

The disadvantages of wholesaling are that you may not have the space to store the stock, nor the physical capacity to handle orders, and these problems of fulfilling wholesale orders may divert staff from the main activities of the trading company. If you are selling wholesale, unless you limit sales to certain specific outlets, such as other museums or specific department stores, you may find that your products are sold in conjunction with products you do not wish to be associated with. You may guard against this by wholesaling only to 'end users' — that is not to any intermediary company. (Ask people where your products will be sold before you agree to supply them). If your products are available outside your museum shop then it can be argued you are lessening your one great trading advantage of exclusivity. The strength of this argument depends on how many customers you actually attract — if your museum is located in the countryside, and attracts no passing trade, then there seems little point in preserving the shops exclusivity. If you have a chain of shops at various sites (like the National Trust) then there is good reason not to wholesale because customers look forward to visiting the shops for the particular products not available elsewhere.

If you hope to wholesale you must fix a price which allows other shops to sell your products at the same or similar prices as you sell the goods in your museum shop. You must supply at a price which allows for the standard mark-up levels for that particular category of item — for gift items this will be 100% + VAT and for books 50%. If you cannot offer goods at these levels of discount then you cannot expect to sell successfully. Why should anyone want to buy your products at 10% discount when they can get 50% or 35% from other suppliers? Are your products so overwhelmingly attractive? If other retailers are prepared to cut their profit margins it is unlikely to be on your goods. If they are cutting profit margins it is more likely to be on the goods they have originated themselves. Consider who might be interested in buying specific products from you. There may be a very few, obvious customers who should be contacted directly. This is probably best done by telephoning to see if they would be interested, and offering to send samples, or prototypes, if available. If you think your product has general appeal, then think about where the retailers you are trying to contact, buy their stock. Is it at trade shows? If so, which? Do they respond to mailings which include samples? Do they read about products in trade journals? If so which journals? Do they rely on travelling salesmen, like an 18th century farmer's wife waiting for the pedlar? It is unlikely that you are able to know exactly how your target market of retailers buy, but thinking about it will certainly give you some ideas. You will also decide which ways of selling you could, in fact, handle. It is no good deciding that your most effective way of reaching your market would be to show at the Spring Fair in Birmingham when the costs are likely to be all-in around £3,000–£4,000 and you neither have the resources nor could depend on generating enough business to hope to recover these costs. (It is interesting that when museums have shown at the Spring Fair and one can think of three of four that have, none have done more than established what they term 'useful contacts' and received levels of orders that have scarcely covered the overheads. None have consistently exhibited, which tells much about their assessment of the venture).

The simplest way of contacting prospective retailers is to circulate them by letter, preferably with a sample, and sample price list, which includes any special terms (such as carriage charges or minimum order levels). It may be worthwhile to follow up your mailing with a quick telephone call, along the lines of 'Have you received the samples we sent and we wondered if you were interested'. Make a note for future use of any contacts and their response. Who should you send your mailing to? You can compile a list of museums and historic houses, with shops, from the annual publications 'Museums and Galleries in Gt. Britain and Ireland' and 'Historic Houses'.

You can reach your target market, perhaps not so effectively, but more simply, by taking an advertisement or paying for a leaflet insert in one of the newsletters which is circulated to the shop managers of those in charge of trading in museums, galleries, cathedrals and historic houses. (A list of the relevant publications is given in the Resources Section). Leaflet inserts may generate orders (make sure you include an order or response form) but are less likely to succeed than if the same information is received by itself, even when directed to the same person. (The direct mail market is constantly tested, since it is devised and run by statisticians and this shows that the effectiveness of inserts declines as the number of them increase – so if yours is one insert of six it is likely to get less response than if it is one of two).

You may decide that you have an ideal product for a particular department store or shop. In which case, contact the buyer and ask if he would be interested and could you send a sample. Try to arrange a meeting. Be persistent if you think the product warrants it. There is a fund of goodwill to museums so you could try the 'I wonder if you could help me, I need your advice' tack. People can rarely resist giving advice when asked, whereas they are quick to harden their hearts if they are being asked to buy something. Do not be ashamed of trying to engage their interest; remember they need new and unusual products to keep their customers interested. That is exactly what you can offer. If they do not want to buy from you, ask them why – is the price wrong, is the product unsuitable, do they think it unattractive? Is it wrong for their market or is it wrong for any market?

When you take orders make sure you can deal with them quickly. Make sure you have the stock. There have been cases of one national museum showing prototypes at Trade Fairs, taking orders, then being unable to fulfil for five months. If delays are likely, warn the customer at the time of ordering: state clearly, for example, 'Available in Spring'. You must be reliable or no one will want to trade with you again. Make sure you can parcel up the orders. Buy in protective packaging. It is time consuming, and therefore costly, to be hunting around for boxes and running out to the corner shop to buy rolls of brown tape. Plan ahead. Make sure you have someone who can make up the parcels. If they are heavy to handle it is no good relying on elderly staff or volunteers. Think how best to arrange delivery. The Post Office can offer a range of special parcel delivery schemes, and special discounts for bulk, as can various road hauliers. Certainly make sure you have the parcels collected, as taking them to the Post Office is time-wasting. Build in all the costs of fulfilling your orders in the wholesale price, then you will not grumble or feel bad tempered about the carriage charges or cost of string.

Remember to invoice for the goods you supply, and chase non-payers with reminders. It is amazing how bad museums are at collecting the money owed them. Remember that money owing is costing you foregone interest.

Once you have established contacts with other retailers, and are geared up to wholesaling, you should try to maintain the impetus. Devise new products with your wholesale market in mind. Wholesaling is like having a shop, once you have it you should try to keep it going. Too often museums will try to wholesale in fits and starts;

128

one year they try then they let it lapse, and the success of the whole operation is doomed. Because the wholesaling is not as public as the shop, does not mean it can be neglected. If you are going to wholesale do it seriously and consistently, but as with all aspects of your trading do review the whole operation and see if it is cost effective.

Shops within shops

In the last decade there has been a change in the organisation of department stores, often as a last ditch attempt by foundering stores to stop the slide into insolvency, by letting out or franchising areas of their shop to various companies, which whilst agreeing to conform to certain design standards in keeping with the store, run their designated area autonomously in terms of stock. There may be a straight rental agreement or the 'shop' within the shop may pay a percentage of turnover, or a combination of both. Some museums have been tempted to experiment with shops within shops – some have been given rent free space, because the department store had a director sympathetic to the museum, and saw it as a way of helping; or the department store has believed the museum's presence could act as a promotional tool to draw customers into the store, or the store has felt it a good way to show its goodwill and community spirit. For its part the museum has usually welcomed the opportunity to expose its merchandise (and its museum) to a wider market, and has had expectations of substantial sales and thus considerable profits.

Those museums that have had shops within stores have generally been disapppointed by the results. Of course, the site for the shop given by the department store has never been very good. It is generally tucked away from the main customer thoroughfares. The harsh commercial reality is that no museum shop is going to generate the level of sales that a department store would expect from its best selling areas. If the museum shop is drawing supporters into the store then it is argued that they will seek it out, asking the floor staff where the 'X' museum promotion is, and the department store hopes that those customers will be tempted en route by the displays of perfume, or toiletries or fabrics or fashions. In its out of the way position the museum shop within a shop is almost doomed to have a

129

forlorn atmosphere about it, which deters customers. Two museums invited to mount displays of merchandise at different times, at Harrods, did not cover the cost of the exercise, and they were given the space free.

It has been usual for museums tempted into these shops within shops to undertake it for a short time and retreat with their tails between their legs. The National Trust has been more consistently maintaining its presence in a few department stores, and hoping to build up its trade by its continued presence. This is completely consistent with the National Trust trading policy which develops product ranges along tried and tested patterns, giving the customers products similar to what they have chosen previously, but in different styles of packaging. The customers know what type of merchandise they can expect in a National Trust shop, and will seek out the shop precisely for that reason. The great advantage to the National Trust of shops within stores is that they are open all year round (whereas the Trust shops at its properties are usually open only part of the year). Department stores are in centres of population, whereas the National Trust's properties and their shops are usually in the countryside, so the shops within stores bring the merchandise to the customers, rather than relying on the customers seeking out the merchandise. It is interesting that the Trust is also opening shops, outside its properties, in historic towns, such as Windsor and Bath, at a rate of 3 or 4 a year.

For most museums their product range is not strong enough to perform well when placed in the context of a department store, in the midst of competing products. When found in the museum shop the product is enhanced by its relevance to the visitor's experience of the museum, and wish to buy a souvenir of the visit. Will the product be sufficiently attractive in its own right to appeal to the general shopper? Are there enough products to create a range of goods, with its concomitant impact. (Ranges of products are particularly sought after by those stocking department stores because they can make a strong visual impact and focus customer attention). Are your products carrying a sufficiently high profit margin to cover the cost of the exercise? You may be able to operate profitably on 50% mark-ups on some items in your museum shop, but the additional costs of the operation in the department store may make this completely unviable. You may have to work on *average* profit margins of 150%, and this may make your goods uncompetitive in

130

price. Generally though, museums have been rather reluctant to price their goods as highly as the market will bear, and certainly there is an argument for having slightly differential pricing, at a lower level in the museum shop and a higher level in other outlets. If the customer discovers the disparity then they have the incentive of visiting the museum shop.

If your museum is offered free space at a department store, ask yourself the following questions (and answer them honestly).

1. Is this a diversion from your humdrum everyday work?
2. Could your energy be better directed to affairs more central to the museum's trading operation.
3. Is a shop within a shop part of your overall strategy (long term or short term)?
4. What will it cost?
5. What can you expect to earn?
6. Will your merchandise when put in the context of a department store damage or enhance your reputation?
7. Should you refuse the offer, but plan to be able to participate in a few years time?

and one personal question

8. Do you reject every proposal because you are lazy, so find excuses for inertia?

Mail order

More and more museums are moving into the area of mail order. Most of the major museums now produce mail order catalogues, many of them quite rudimentary, but increasingly, of such sophistication one wonders how they can afford the production costs.

Mail order is important in reaching new customers. It also has the advantage of extending the selling season (most usually museum shops are at their busiest in the summer, and the museum's mail-order catalogue will hopefully stimulate out of season trade, generally pre-Christmas). The catalogue may stimulate visits to the museum shop, because it makes people aware of new, exciting items, or indeed of the very existence of the shop itself. Many people like receiving mail order catalogues. Their pleasure may not extend to buying anything, however. Remember that impulse buying in the shop, which may account for many purchases, especially of gift and souvenir items, will not apply to the mail order catalogue, where the effort and time needed to write out the order and cheque act as a brake on impulse! That is why mail order catalogue producers encourage potential customers to telephone orders in, using a credit card, for immediate gratification!

As well as the mail order catalogues of individual museums there are now several catalogues based on goods from a number of museums and galleries. Sometimes not all the products derive from museums, but all are chosen to look as if they did. For example, there may be replicas, stationery items with pseudo art nouveau designs and reproductions of Staffordshire pottery! These types of catalogues reflect the retail trend toward theme shopping, and are directed towards a particular type of customer who are hopefully pre-selected for their interest in this type of merchandise.

Any museum wanting to have its items sold via these special catalogues of museum goods should approach the compilers, with their suggested items. The economics of mail order are such that you must be prepared to supply at good discount. Most museums have been surprised, and disappointed, at the relatively small quantities which are actually sold through these general catalogues.

Those compiling the catalogue usually take a small initial quantity, to cover first orders, from which they gauge the likely demand, and on which to base their re-order. If the response is good there will be a large re-order, if it is small there may be no re-order at all. The museum supplying the goods are expected to be able to respond quickly to the demand for re-orders. In a sense, the supplier is carrying the risk by having the stock available on demand. Generally it is not worth taking any additional risk of having extra stock on the off-chance of a mail order catalogue re-ordering in substantial quantities. This of course, depends on the size of the mail order catalogue in which the product is featured, but certainly seems to be sound advice for the current mail order catalogues offering general museum ranges. If the mail order catalogue company thinks a product is a sure fire success they will give a substantial initial order. If you make clear that you do not hold back-up stock (and they should, if they are competent, have enquired about this from the start) and how long it would take to re-supply, you should be able to work out a mutually satisfactory strategy – perhaps on the basis that they would guarantee to take a specified proportion of any newly ordered stock from the museum, though possibly with deferred payment.

Checklist for those planning a mailorder catalogue

Products

What would you sell?
Are these items easy to send by post?
Do you have these items in stock?
Could you re-order quickly?
Will the item be easy to illustrate in a catalogue?
Can the items be grouped for the catalogue? (i.e. do they relate to each other?)
What profit margins can you achieve a) overall
                                               b) on each item

Catalogue production

Who will produce your catalogue
  a) design layout
  b) photography
  c) print
How many will you produce?
What will it cost?
How does this work per catalogue, per projected order?

Distribution of the catalogue

How will you distribute your catalogue?
Do you have a mailing list (and are those on it likely to respond?)
Can you borrow other lists, or buy them?
How good are such lists likely to be?
Who will handle the actual mail out (in-house, or by a mailing house?)

Publicity

What is your budget for publicity?
How will you spend it?

Fulfilment

How will you fulfil orders? (in-house or use a fulfilment house?)
Can you respond quickly enough?
If you use a fulfilment house how will you find one?
How will you ensure the fulfilment house is efficient?
How will you deal with out of stock items – refund or split order?
Have you arranged special rates with The Post Office (who offer generous rebates) for mail order?
Are you charging enough for post and packaging to cover your actual costs. Is this level a deterrent to potential customers?

Finances

How will you pay for initial stock (can you arrange credit from your suppliers?)
How will you pay for your catalogues production and distribution costs? (NB mail order catalogues inevitably need substantial initial capital)
Have you worked out the necessary order levels to:
a) cover costs
b) make profits
Is it realistic to think you will recover your costs of catalogue production and mailing by the sales generated?

Other possible benefits

Can you convert new customers to regular supporters (Friends of the Museum).
How are you keeping records of purchasers (remember, you will want to mail them in future).

And one final question:

Are you going into mail order for sound commercial reasons, or just because you feel it adds status to your trading?

Mail Order
Selina Fellows, *Royal Academy*

I hope by this brief outline of the development of the RA's Gift Catalogue to describe and answer some of the questions to be taken into consideration when discussing a mail order or direct mail programme.

R. A. Enterprises Limited (the trading company affiliated to the Academy) has four profit centres; the Shop, the Mail Order Catalogue, the Restaurant and the Framing service. The Mail Order Gift Catalogue was originated in 1981 with the primary purpose of increasing sales revenue. Another factor was the wish to establish a profit centre which was separate from the retail operation.

The great incentive for the Academy was the existence of the mailing list (in excess of 25,000 Friends of the Royal Academy). The areas through which we can trace our development are the mailing list, the product, production of the Gift Catalogue, order fulfilment and results. Before discussing any of these we had first to look at the size and scope of operation which we were considering and I spent some time talking to the heads of various charity and commercial mail order catalogues. At that time (1980) the mail order sales area was still recovering from some fairly drastic knocks to its image. Now, however, bodies such as the British Direct Mail Association (BDMA) and the Mail Order Protection Scheme (MOPS) have to a large extent re-assured the public and developed, if not a trust, at least an understanding of purchasing by post. It is unlikely that the U. K. market will ever be able to rival the U. S. for sheer size and variety of catalogues, but mail order has become an established purchasing pattern. It goes without saying that any charity or institution must be above criticism in the handling of orders as the implications spread further – for example into donor giving etc. It is essential to see the venture as 100% professional and seek as much advice as necessary at the outset.

MAILING LIST

The list of Friends of the Royal Academy is stored on computer and geo-coded for postal rebates. Our list is relatively small beside some of the larger charities who mail hundreds of thousands of supporters, rather than thousands. We have expanded out list over the years so that it is not only composed of 'live' Friends of the R. A., but also of names acquired in various other ways.

One of the most popular methods of adding names is to buy a list. There are lists of names for virtually any section of the population which one wants to target-mail. The BDMA have a list of reputable List Brokers and it may be useful to talk to them. Buying lists is a relatively expensive means of acquiring names (expect to pay £45 to £55 per 1,000 on 1986 prices for good names) but if the right list is bought it can yield reasonably profitable results. An alternative is to swap a list of names with another charity or institution or whatever. This has the big advantage that the names are 'free' – however they will probably not be as well profiled as a purchased list. One should also beware of duplicating names when swapping and it is probably worth investing in a 'merge and purge' which will extract any names which may already be on your list. The cheapest means of acquiring names is to print some slips for retail customers to fill their names and addresses in on if they want a copy of the mail order catalogue. These slips can either be left beside a till in the Shop or put into the bags of all customers who purchase over a certain value of goods. These names will probably yield a relatively high response rate. Once the catalogue is established a number of names can be added to the list from requests by the general public. It is worth coding all the different names by source from the outset, in order to measure response at a later date, as it may not be profitable mailing to certain names. For example the customer who wrote and asked to be included on the mailing list, but has not bought anything after two mail shots can then be deleted. It is also worth contacting the BDMA and MOPS to ensure that any legal requirements are complied with.

The actual cost of mailing is high and obviously should be kept as low as possible. The first and most obvious point we checked was the actual weight of the mailing – including the envelope – as a gram or two can push the charge into a higher postal band. The Post Office's marketing department has altered radically over the last few years and their representatives are now keen to advise the customer on the best use that is available from the service. It is possible to negotiate a special rate for geo-coded bulk mailings and also for parcel quantities.

The Royal Academy's Gift Catalogue is always sent out with the Friends magazine i.e. a piggy-back mailing and this saves a lot of money if the combined weight stays within the selected postal charge band. We have done a couple of test mail shots in the past to swapped

136

names and as well as the Gift Catalogue have included details of membership to the Friends of the Royal Academy and the Appeal – both have had a good response.

The development and use of a list is a specialist area and it may be worth talking to a direct mail consultant in order to assess the potential for development.

PRODUCT

A product which sells well in the Shop does not necessarily sell well by mail order. The best example of this for us is books, which account for a reasonable amount of our retail revenue. However when we tried to sell them by mail order they did not achieve a similar percentage of turnover. This was probably because of the postage and packing costs, which were too high on a product which was relatively easily obtainable from a local bookshop. It is also noteworthy that some products do not photograph as well as they display (for example postcards look far more tempting in our Shop than in the mail order catalogue) and vice versa (for example clothing can be demonstrated and modelled to greater effect in a photograph).

A product which is exclusive or not readily available elsewhere will probably sell best. Most of our range fits the former category. We offer items from about £1.50 to £50. Many of the large charity mail order catalogues have a large range of 'pocket money' priced items, but this is a reflection of their customer profile. The Academy catalogue and products are aimed at a customer who is willing to pay for something of quality or unusual and of a good design and visual standard.

When we decided to start a mail order catalogue a small advisory panel was set up which included a designer, a retailer and a journalist. This panel was extremely useful as an informed and impartial view on the type of product and style we were developing. The Academy Catalogue is almost exclusively devoted to our own originated product and a reasonable amount of our resources are spent on this. A spin off from this has been the growth of our wholesale sales.

Useful events for the developing and sourcing of product are the Birmingham Gift Fair (at the NEC, in the first week of February) and Top Drawer (April & September in London). There are many other trade fairs and a Chamber of Commerce will have details of dates of any local ones. We have found trade fairs useful for product ideas and for finding manufacturers — particularly for small quantity orders to a special design. We aim to have final samples in May (to be photographed in June) and delivery of stock early August. Delivery periods for any re-orders during the busy pre-Christmas period are agreed at the time of the placement of the initial order, so that we do not run out of stock.

PRODUCTION OF CATALOGUE

The costs involved in putting together a mail order catalogue can be as large or as small as one wishes to pay for the style of presentation sought. The basic costs are a photographer (or illustrator), a designer and a printer. We put out for quotations for all of these and encourage a rapport between the three people involved in order to avoid any costly mistakes. We start photography in early June and give copy and transparencies to the designer two weeks later who in turn produces finished artwork for the printer by the beginning of July, who in turn produces the finished and printed catalogue by mid August for mailing at the end of the month.

Our first catalogue was a colour A5 eight page fold-out and over the years we have progressed to 24 page A5 (8 pages of colour, 12 pages of black and white and 4 of order forms). From the outset we wanted to create our own style, and look.

Print buying can be a job in itself. Again it depends upon what sort of job one is looking for. If the catalogue is being developed from scratch it is unlikely that the print run will be six figures or the job a 48 page colour brochure. Very likely it could be a one colour print job on a folded A4 sheet. One of the most financially successful New York museum catalogues was an imaginative use of line drawings and sepia photographs in a 24 page book.

ORDER FULFILMENT

Legally, an order has to be turned around in 28 days, however it is important to process the order as quickly as possible as a customer will often count from the day the order was posted. It may also be worth setting up a telephone ordering system as more and more customers prefer to use the telephone for credit card ordering.

We investigated a number of mail order houses as we do not have a large despatch department at the Academy. It is essential to have an efficient and reliable system where queries and orders are speedily despatched. *The cost of fulfilment can either be built into the product price or shown as part of the postage and packing costs. It is normal for a fulfilment house to make a charge for order handling (i.e. dealing with post, banking money etc) on top of the cost of packing materials, labour and postage.*

RESULTS

Table A shows how an outline feasibility study for the financial implications of a mail order catalogue. As well as financial benefits there may be other intangible benefits such as promotion and increased awareness of the institution and its work. We sent out a reply paid questionnaire about the mail order catalogues asking recipients various questions. About 50% of our mailing list live in the London area (i.e. easily accessible to the Royal Academy) and a very high proportion of responders said that they use the catalogue to browse through – rather than purchasing by post they choose what they want and buy it on their next visit to the Academy.

In the final analysis there are three factors which determine the success of a mail order catalogue – selling the right products at the right prices to the right mailing list.

Table A

INCOME
  % response of list = number of orders
  Average order value

EXPENDITURE
  Extra staff costs
  Photography
  Design
  Printing
  Postage for catalogue
    (assumed order postage costs passed to customers)
  Fulfilment costs
  Costs of names for mailing list
  Extra stock investment

Table B

Royal Academy of Arts Gift Catalogue

We have now published five Gift Catalogues and it would be helpful for us to know your reaction to them.

We should be very grateful if you would complete and return this short questionnaire. The postage is pre-paid so no stamp is necessary.

Please tick the appropriate boxes:

1. **Did you receive the 1984 Gift Catalogue in time to use it for your Christmas shopping?** YES ☐ NO ☐

2. **Have you bought anything shown in the Catalogue?**

   ☐ (a) yes—used the mail order service
   ☐ (b) saw something in it which I bought direct from the Royal Academy Shop
   ☐ (c) haven't bought anything yet, but intend to do so
   ☐ (d) have not bought and do not intend to do so

3. **There are a number of reasons why people might not use the Catalogue. Please indicate which of the following apply to you:**

   ☐ (a) selection of items not attractive
   ☐ (b) range of items not wide enough
   ☐ (c) prices of items too high
   ☐ (d) cost of postage too high
   ☐ (e) do not like purchasing items by post
   ☐ (f) any other reason – please specify

   _____

   _____

4. **Do you think we should continue to provide a Gift Catalogue?**

   ☐ (a) yes – with mail order facilities
   ☐ (b) yes – but with goods only available from Royal Academy Shop
   ☐ (c) no – discontinue gift catalogue

5. **Are you a Friend of the Royal Academy?** YES ☐ NO ☐

6. **Which county or town do you live in?** *(This information is for market research so we do not need to know your name or full address.)*

   _____

Thank you very much for completing the questionnaire. If you have any other comments (for example suggestions of items you would like to see in the next Gift Catalogue) please write them below.

_____

_____

Useful Addresses

BDMA (British Direct Mail Association)
1 New Oxford Street, London WC1 Tel: 242 2254.

MOPS (Mail Order Protection Scheme)
Newspaper Publishers Association, 16 Tooks Court, London
EC4A 1LB.

Exporting to America

Leon Yow: *UK Museums Marketing Group of the Charities Advisory Trust.*

The museum stores of the USA beckon like a temptress to museum traders of the UK. The museum store in America is more highly developed than its UK counterpart, with high sales levels, and as such can sell an item in larger quantities than most UK counterparts. This makes the prospect of selling goods for resale in American museum shops particularly attractive. A substantial trade order is the ideal of all wholesalers, and the American museum stores, with their large turnovers seem to offer the possibility of such orders.

In 1985 the UK Museum Marketing Group, an initiative of the Charities Advisory Trust, undertook a feasibility study to see whether exporting to the USA was in fact a viable proposition for UK museums. A range of products was compiled, trade prices worked out and samples packed. These were displayed fairly informally at the Museum Stores Association Annual Convention. (Prior research had shown that this was the principal venue for buying for museum stores in the USA). Though customers were queuing at the stall throughout the day, this pilot study highlighted key problem areas.

1. **Pricing:** *It was clear that prices would have to be quoted that were firm. One could not expect orders on the basis of the fluctuating values of the pound and dollar. You have to make a judgement on likely currency fluctuations and be aware that this could make or break the profitability of the whole operation. If you are over cautious and allow too generously for any rise in the value of the pound, you are likely to price your goods too highly.*

2. **Customs:** *Customs duties are charged at varying rates on imports to the USA. The British Overseas Trade Board is very helpful, and will provide a list of all the rates. The customs dues cannot be pre-paid, so the customer in the USA is going to be charged customs on receipt of the parcel (as well as a small customs handling fee). If you want to quote a final price – including the customs, this means you will be involved in very complicated calculations on the insurance, postage cost, net value etc, to get a figure on which customs is due. Though*

tempting to make it as easy as possible for the customer, and so quote an 'all-in price' it does increase the time needed to process orders to an uneconomic degree. It is probably better to quote a price including carriage but excluding customs though you can give the customer a clear idea of levels of import duties for example, 5.6% on greetings cards + $2.50 customs handling. There are companies which will in fact handle all the customs forms and paperwork for you and this might be an attractive alternative.

3. **Small orders:** *Although the US museums may have a high turnover of sales, experience shows they like to order little and often. (The average order from US museum stores is likely to be around $300 – and that is where a minimum of $250 was imposed!) This works against the exporter, who because of the high freight costs, and complexity of processing orders, cannot handle small orders economically. Also the habit of small orders with many repeats, shows a method of buying which relies on repeat calls and reminders, for which the exporter may not be set up. (He can only afford an annual visit, and so misses the sales opportunities throughout the year).*

4. **Agents:** *Since US museum stores order little and often, the best way of selling may be to use an agent, who will, as well as exhibiting at trade shows, make calls and cultivate likely buyers. Many of those exhibiting at the Museum Stores Association Trade Show are agents, and they are eager for additional 'lines'. It would be easy enough to find a suitable agent. The Tate Gallery after exporting directly to the USA for some years now uses an agent. Items can be shipped over in bulk to the agent and distributed directly. This reduces the costs of shipping, and a great deal of the trouble of processing export orders, with their complicated documentation. Using an agent has many advantages. The customer museum in the USA also likes to have a US phone number and address to call with any queries, and an agent provides one! The disadvantages of an agent is that prices will increase. The agent expects to make a living from selling your products. To do so he will increase the prices. It is ironic that a UK museum will complain bitterly at the uneconomic costs of processing orders to the US, yet fail to increase the price sufficiently to compensate itself. As soon as it*

143

hands over to an agent he puts the price up beyond what the museum would consider. Does this matter, has it led to a fall in sales? Generally, UK museum goods are competitively priced for the US market. Also, UK museum goods carry a cachet, enhancing both the reputation of the museum or origin and the vendor museum, and the goods can be priced highly and still sell.

5. **Delivery schedules.** *American museum shops have high delivery standards. Orders are often given stipulating a cancellation date if goods are not received by a cut-off date. To meet these demands museums and galleries wanting to be involved in exporting may well have to redeploy their resources to make allowances for additional staff.*

6. **What goods sell best?** *Paper goods of all types from publications through to greetings cards, are competitively priced for the American market. Facsimiles, for example of Cruikshank's caricature 'The Toothache' are popular, as are reproductions of Victorian pop-up greeting cards. Somewhat surprisingly, American museum shops have significant sales of inexpensive jewellery, so there is a demand for replicas.*

   Generally British goods are competitively priced, but textiles, such as tea towels are expensive compared with their American counterparts. Toys and children's items from the UK are competing in America not with US made goods but with cheap imports from the Far East. Unless the product is very distinctive it will not stand up well in this mass market.

7. **Provenance cards.** *The requirements of the American Inland Revenue Service means that museum shops can only stock what is relevant to its collection and/or educational. It is therefore helpful to the museum shop in America to be supplied with a provenance card, explaining what the product is, its origin and relevance to the museum.*

8. **Import regulations.** *Whilst it is not impossible to export cosmetics and food products to the USA, there are stringent labelling requirements. Unless you are going to export a great deal of any one item it may not be worthwhile to try to export as you will not want to incur the expense of special labelling. If you haven't got your labelling right the goods will be impounded by the US Customs.*

9. **Payment.** *American customers will want to pay in dollars, with a cheque drawn on their bank. Such cheques can be paid into a British bank account, but you will pay a high handling charge for each transaction. It is easy to open a dollar account in a bank in America (your own British bank will almost certainly have American branches, and can arrange for you to open a dollar account at one). Then when receiving US dollar cheques you simply pay them into the American bank. Transfer the money back to your own UK bank account as you wish. One very positive advantage of exporting to American museum shops – they are generally prompt payers!*

Statistical Information on Museum Trading

It is as difficult for museum trading as for any type of commercial activity to collect hard facts. Too often those concerned 'hype' their facts, exaggerating successes, and writing off failures as public relations exercises, or attributing them to interference by the museum's director. Where the museum's trading is carried out by a separate company one can consult the annual accounts, lodged by law at Companies House. These provide a useful check, but are not always as informative as they might be.

One problem with museum trading is that one is not always comparing like with like. The museum shop that offers a real educational service to visitors will be less profitable than one which simply offers a range of souvenirs stamped with the museum's name. Profitability can only be gauged against an informed background.

The two analyses that follow provide interesting insights into the trading of museums. The statistics from Data Base, backed up by the Yorkshire and Humberside study, give an interesting overall view of museum trading in the UK, showing that whilst most museums had some form of trading, the scale was very small.

Thomas Aageson's study of museum stores in the USA is a very useful analysis, which has much to offer those involved in museum trading in this country, most significantly because it shows what type of information to collect to make financial analysis possible, but also because it shows the ranges in performance. It becomes possible for the individual museum shop to set itself targets, which have been achieved in other museum shops.

146

Statistical information on museum trading derived from the Museum Association's Data-Base

The Museum Association's Data-Base project from 1983–86 has amassed statistical information on museums in the UK. Some of this relates to the museums' trading and we have abstracted the relevant figures.

It is apparent from the figures that we are not always looking at exactly the same set of museums and this should be borne in mind, since it implies that the consistency required for completely reliable interpretation of the statistics is lacking.

Because not all museums answering the Data-Base questionnaire gave information on trading, the figures are given as percentages.

Sales points

79% of the sample did have shops or sales points of some kind.

Guidebooks

52% of the sample had their own guidebooks.

Turnover per annum

The following tables show firstly overall turnover (ie sales) levels in a sample of 450 museum shops and sales points (Table 1), and then a

Table 1 Overall sales

Value of retail turnover (£)	Percentage	Cumulative percentage
2,500 or less per annum	73.6	73.6
2,501–10,000	14.0	87.6
10,001–50,000	8.0	95.6
50,001–125,000	2.2	97.8
125,001–250,000	0.4	98.2
250,001–750,000	1.6	99.8
750,001–1,000,000	0.2	100.0
Total	100.0	

147

Table 2 Sales of museums' own goods

Value of sales (£)	Percentage	Cumulative percentage
50 or less	35.6	35.6
51–100	5.0	40.6
101–500	17.3	57.9
501–1,000	8.5	66.4
1,001–5,000	18.7	85.1
5,001–10,000	5.6	90.7
10,001–50,000	6.1	96.8
50,001–100,000	1.8	98.6
100,001–200,000	0.6	99.2
200,001–300,000	0.6	99.8
Above 300,000	0.2	100.0
Total	100.0	

breakdown of this into three distinct categories: sales of the museums' own goods (Table 2), sales of other publications (Table 3), and finally sales of food and drink (Table 4).

Please note, with all these statistics, that the classes used are not always equal.

The most notable fact is that about three-quarters of those museums giving information on trading had retail turnover of less than £2,500.

It is interesting to note that such a high percentage clearly sell only their own goods, and one assumes that this is usually a limited range

Table 3 Sales of other publications

Value of sales (£)	Percentage	Cumulative percentage
0	72.9	72.9
1–50	1.8	74.7
51–100	1.3	76.0
101–500	6.0	82.0
501–1,000	4.4	86.4
1,001–5,000	7.1	93.5
5,001–10,000	3.0	96.5
10,001–50,000	2.2	98.7
50,001–100,000	0.4	99.1
100,001–200,000	0.5	99.6
Above 200,000	0.4	100.0
Total	100.0	

Table 4 Sales of food and drink

Value of sales (£)	Percentage	Cumulative percentage
0	85.2	85.2
1–50	1.4	86.6
51–100	0.8	87.4
101–500	4.1	91.5
501–1,000	0.9	92.4
1,001–5,000	3.3	95.7
5,001–10,000	1.0	96.7
10,001–50,000	2.2	98.9
Above 50,000	1.1	100.0
Total	100.0	

of postcards, guide books and possibly souvenir pens and book-marks, specially produced with the museum's own name or logo.

Less than 15% had any revenue from catering.

Staffing

The figures here show 88% of the sample to have had no sales staff, 5% to have had one member of staff, $2\frac{1}{2}$% two members of staff, $1\frac{1}{2}$% three members of staff and a negligible proportion more than three staff.

The public relations and publicity work that could be used to promote the museums' trading was even less well staffed, 96% having no such staff and 3% having one or two.

The fact that only 12% employed any staff to man their shops or run their trading shows that, overall, the scale of trading is very low. In practice, warding staff will in many cases deal with sales as they arise – there are no figures to show any apportionment of time for these duties, so presumably they are negligible (or the museum would have indicated a part-time apportionment.)

Proportion of the cost of the retailing operation as a proportion of the museum's overall expenditure

Not surprisingly, since most museums do not operate retailing operations on a scale to even employ staff, the cost of the museum's trading operation is an insignificant part of its overall budget, as the following table clearly shows.

149

Table 5 Gross retail expenditure as a percentage of total expenditure

Value (%)	Percentage	Cumulative percentage
0	44.9	44.9
0.01–7.5	33.5	78.4
7.51–10	2.5	80.9
10.01–50	17.7	98.6
More than 50	1.4	100.0
Total	100.0	

Retail Turnover by Visitor Numbers

It is interesting (see Table 6) that there is not more correlation between retail turnover (sales in the museum shop) and the number of visitors. This carries the implication that the museums are not making the most of their selling opportunities!

Table 6 Retail Turnover by Visitor Numbers (Grouped)

	Total number of visits			
	5,000 or less	5,001 to 10,000	10,001 to 50,000	Over 50,000
Turnover in retailing (£)	Percentage	Percentage	Percentage	Percentage
2,500 or less	24.6	16.5	24.1	4.2
2,501–10,000	1.4	1.7	9.5	4.2
Over 10,000	0.6	0	2.5	10.6

Stastical information on museum trading derived from the Visitor Spending Survey of the Museum and Art Gallery Service for Yorkshire and Humberside

A similar type of survey was carried out for the museums and art galleries in Yorkshire and Humberside, by the Museum and Art Gallery Service for Yorkshire and Humberside. This survey had a better response rate but portrayed a similar picture.

Of those institutions replying to the questionnaire, 85% had some kind of sales point (only 32% having what they would actually refer to as a shop). Of those institutions with sales points, only 6% had paid sales staff, 84% being run by attendants, and the remainder by volunteers.

Table 7 Retail turnover (sales)

Value of sales (£)	Percentage	Cumulative percentage
0–250	38.7	38.7
251–500	3.2	41.9
501–750	9.7	51.6
751–1,000	6.5	58.1
1,001–2,000	9.7	67.8
2,001–3,000	6.5	74.3
3,001–4,000	6.5	80.8
4,001–5,000	3.2	84.0
5,001–10,000	6.4	90.4
10,001–20,000	3.2	93.6
20,001–30,000	3.2	96.8
More than 30,000	3.2	100.0
Total	100.0	

Turnover (sales) varied from about £20 per annum to over £60,000 per annum. Table 7 shows how the museums surveyed were dispersed across this range; and it is interesting to note the consistency with the national figures on turnover, with about three-quarters of the sample having retail turnover value of less than £2,500.

Table 8 relates selling operations to numbers of visitors to the institutions and, as in the case of the national survey, such analysis does not show as much positive correlation as might be expected, i.e. low exploitation of selling opportunities relative to potential.

Of the busiest 12 institutions (of which one had over half a million visitors, two had over 200,000 visitors and 9 had over 100,000 visitors) only half had a shop, only three had specialist sales staff and

Table 8 Retail Turnover by Visitor Numbers (Grouped) in Yorkshire and Humberside

	Total number of visits			
	5,000 or less	5,001 to 10,000	10,001 to 50,000	Over 50,000
Turnover in retailing (£)	Percentage	Percentage	Percentage	Percentage
2,500 or less	24.2	3.0	33.3	15.2
2,501–10,000	0	0	3.0	12.1
Over 10,000	0	0	0	9.2

amazingly only two claimed that the scale of their selling operations should be bigger. Four of the twelve returned no sales income at all.

Financial Information on Museum Stores in America, abstracted from Thomas Aageson: Financial Analysis for Museum Stores (1986)

Thomas Aageson's Sales Analysis Workshops are a regular feature of the Museums Stores Association of America's Annual Convention. Aaegeson has collected financial data from 197 participating

FINANCIAL SUMMARY BY MUSEUM TYPE

	Type of Museum				
	Childrens	Art	Science	History	Other
Number of Stores					
< $125,000 Sales	3	44	35	35	8
> $125,000 Sales	2	32	33	21	5
Inventory Turn	2.1	2.0	1.6	1.7	1.9
Gross Profit	43.0%	45.0%	44.0%	45.0%	46.5%
Square Footage	1,025	742	861	625	674
Attendance					
< $125,000 Sales	22,000	61,500	65,000	50,000	43,000
> $125,000 Sales	320,000	289,000	607,000	129,000	160,000
Sales Per Visitor					
< $125,000 Sales	$0.15	$0.69	$0.61	$1.01	$1.51
> $125,000 Sales	$0.42	$1.56	$0.76	$1.65	$2.59
Sales Per Sq. Ft.					
< $125,000 Sales	$37	$101	$83	$116	$105
> $125,000 Sales	$160	$302	$249	$234	$114
Visitors Per Sq. Ft.					
< $125,000 Sales	135	121	132	112	89
> $125,000 Sales	668	213	394	146	115

All data is the median performance for each category.
  < $125,000 Sales = Stores with Sales Up to $125,000
  > $125,000 Sales = Stores with Sales Exceeding $125,000
NOTE: Totals greater than total sample combined museums were included twice (Nature Center and Art Museum treated as two museums).

museum stores and presents it in his book 'Financial Analysis for Museum Stores'. The figures are for the period 1980–83 inclusive.

The most significant of Aageson's findings can be summarised thus:

1. **Basically museum stores are small business,** only 10% of the sample had sales over $500,000.

2. **Low attendance does not mean a small sales volume.**

3. **Size of the store** – typically stores were small – over half had under 750 square feet.

N.B. The larger the store the greater the sales volume. The physical size of the store is a better indication of sales volume than attendance. Intense crowding keeps sales down.

4. **Sales per square foot.**

Sales per square foot (i.e. related to size of shop) showed the following range:

Stores with sales up to $125,000 – sales per square foot ranged $6–628

Stores with sales above $125,000 – sales per square foot ranged $55–2,156

5. **Sales per visitor.**

Range 5c–$16.11c

Sales per visitor are affected by the relative size of the store in relationship to attendance.

9 out of 10 stores with exceptionally low sales per visitor are Science Museums. This is because visitors are mainly schoolchildren, also the shops are small.

'Stores which have a relatively low ratio of visitors per square foot are more conducive to merchandising higher price point merchandise. . . . Larger stores can often offer more lines of merchandise and meet the needs of more visitors, which increases sales per visitor as well.'

6. **Visitors per square foot** – comparison of compact and open museum stores.

Compact store – 200 visitors per square foot
Open store   – 50 visitors per square foot

Compact stores tend to be self-service and carry lower priced merchandise.

153

Compact stores achieve higher sales per square foot by over 200%, but have smaller sales per visitor.

7. Gross margins.
Gross profit has no relationship to how fast inventory turns over in a store. . . . Stores with high gross profit can have high or low stock-turn. There is, however, a tendency for stores with the high sales per square foot to have higher gross profit.
Most stores had gross profits of 40–50% (56% of sample) 10% managed 50–54%. Only 1 managed 70%.

8. Stock-turn.
Stock-turn varied from $\frac{1}{2}$ to 3.
2 stock-turn was therefore the median.
Compared to commercial retailers the museum store was achieving a 2-time stock-turn, retail stores a 3-time.

	Commercial Store	*Museum Store*
Sales	$200,000	$200,000
Cost of Goods	$110,000	$110,000
Gross Profit	$90,000	$90,000
Average Inventory	$36,666	$55,000
Inventory Turn	$\dfrac{\$110,000}{\$36,666} = 3.0$	$\dfrac{\$110,000}{\$55,000} = 2.0$

Aageson believes museum involvement in special products, particularly for exhibitions, slows its stock turn. He advocates excluding from calculation of stock the museum's scholarly publications.

Museum shops abroad

It seems sensible for museum shops in the UK to have some regard to what is going on in the museum shops abroad, since many of its customers are foreign visitors. It can only be helpful to understand what their experience of museum shops at home leads them to expect in museum shops abroad.

In most of the European countries the museum shops are relatively simple counters, with little on sale beyond postcards, slides, some reproductions of pictures, and a range of publications that are often limited to a few scholarly catalogues. At one end of the scale, for example in Italy, museums will have virtually no trading in the museum (although in Florence, for example, the guides to the collections written by the museum director will be on sale at market stalls outside the major galleries, as will a range of postcards and reproductions). The museum's trading is completely left to individual private enterprise, and it is interesting to note just what is offered when commercial criteria are applied! The Italian museums are at one extreme, with very little, if anything, actually offered on sale in the museum. In France the centralisation of museums has resulted in a much extended range of goods derived from disparate museums being offered in many museum shops. In France, there has also been a move towards shops outside the museums (which is outlined subsequently). For most European visitors the museum shops of museums in the UK must seem perfectly adequate, offering a larger selection than they have at home.

One cannot say as much for American visitors, who because of the different role of their museums in the community, may, depending on where they live and visit in the USA, be used to museum shops which can be the size of small department stores, and offer an enormous range of goods. It is not unusual for a museum shop in the USA to provide the best general, and certainly the best children's bookshop in the town. Often the museum shop will specialise in jewellery, crafts or modern design items. (The Crafts Council shop at the Victoria and Albert Museum is less surprising to American visitors than to their British counterparts.) To understand why museum shops in the USA have developed to such a sophisticated level, one has to understand the role of museums in American society. The museum acts as a focal point for a successful section of society, and much of the social life of the upper echelons of society will be centred on the museum, through a series of fund-raising and cultural events organised either by or for the museum. Association with the museum confers social status. This spills over into shopping at the museum shop, and indeed may even involve acting as a volunteer in the museum shop. A significant proportion of American museum shops are not only staffed by volunteer assistants, but are entirely run by volunteers. There are museums and galleries in the UK where the community support and involvement is strong, for example, at the Ferens Gallery in Hull or the Harris Art Gallery in Preston. But although the hope of those running our museums is to build up 'Friends' groups and move towards American style involvement, we certainly are a long way from the American situation. Indeed one wonders if British society in the nineteenth century was not a closer parallel to the current American position. Perhaps we had our period of involvement, and social forces have changed. The Royal Academy has been the most successful at building up support through social activities, and this has been reflected in its profitable trading.

In the last few years there has been a very interesting development in America which may be showing the direction of museum trading in the future. In Boston, a property developer intent on enhancing a prestige shopping mall, set up what is in effect a shop called 'The Gallery of Museums'. Ten leading American museums and galleries were invited to participate. The shop, extremely lavishly designed, sought to reflect the atmosphere of each participating museum, in its display, and sold a range of items from each. The shop was divided into ten separate areas, though the separation was not rigorous, it compared rather with a display by a manufacturer in a department store, and there were common areas in which items for all or several of the museums would be displayed. Antiques, many for sale, were mixed in with the custom made shop fittings, all set to create the appropriate atmosphere. Each month a guest museum was invited to participate, and so ensure something new in the shop each month.

The project has flourished and a chain of galleries of museums is planned. Why has the project been so successful? The participating museums have been able to provide an interesting and unusual range of goods. The role of the museum in American society gives those products a cachet. The customer is buying prestigious gift items which are not commonly available rather than books or scholarly publications. The best selling items at the Gallery of Museum shops are food from Old Sturbridge Village (which are rather like the National Trust's food items), antiques from Salem and the well known gift products from the Metropolitan Museum in New York and the Bostom Museum of Fine Arts. All the participating museums hope to benefit by increasing the number of visitors to their actual museums. Sales through the shop helps them because it mops up the production run, and they benefit financially because the unit cost is reduced by the economies of scale. The museums supply the Gallery of Museums at below normal wholesale prices – production cost plus 20% is the norm. This enables the operation, which is run as a business, not a service, to build in the appropriate profit margins. On the other hand, sales are not on a sale or return basis, but firm sales, and this certainly makes the whole proposition more attractive to participating museums. (There is also the temptation to agree to participate because other reputable museums are doing so and one feels one has to be seen amongst them, and this may in fact outweigh the straight commercial considerations).

The Gallery of Museums may be a new way of selling museum goods that could be replicated in Britain. In France, the centralised administration of museums by the Ministry of Culture has led to the opening up of a series of museum shops in important shopping areas. The shops are very 'up-market', featuring a wide range of reproductions, from replicas of horses' heads through to porcelain and silk scarves. The prices are high. The whole range of merchandise is aimed at the affluent gift buyer, and the interior decorator. There are no leather bookmarks or souvenir pencils here. It is not clear whether these shops are run for profit or cultural prestige, and one suspects the latter is the prime motive. It certainly creates an awareness of museums and their collections (especially since so much of the stock is of large replicas) just as the statuary at the Louvre underground station takes the museum to the people in an attempt to tempt them inside. Both the Gallery of Museums and the chain of French museum shops are interesting visions of what can be done with museum trading.

157

25 Key Questions to be asked by those running museum trading companies

Purpose
  why are we trading?
  do our activities help promote the museum?
  are we a good or bad advertisement for the museum?
  do we expect to make a profit?

Physical
  are we located in the right place?
  is our shop layout and storage efficient?
  do we have adequate space?

Buying
  are we buying cheapest and best?
  are our stock levels too high?
  are our prices too high, too low or about right?
  does our stock reflect our collection?
  do we provide customers with a good range of products?

Organisation and staff
  is our structure appropriate?
  can we respond flexibly to opportunities?
  how good is the age and skills structure of our employees?
  how good is staff morale?
  do we try hard enough?

Finance
  how profitable are we?
  is our budget secure?
  could we borrow for expansion?
  are we at risk financially through high interest rates?

Security
  what are our stock losses, and how does this compare with other
    shops?
  is our financial control tight enough?

Sales and promotion
  do we sell well to customers?
  do we promote and advertise sufficiently?

How are we going to overcome the problems the above questions
have pinpointed?

Resources

Museum trading straddles the museum world and the commercial world. You may want more information on one or the other or perhaps both. This section includes material about both museums and commerce; it is not exhaustive on either, but tries to indicate the direction in which to look for further information.

Organisations which can help

Area Museum Councils

There are nine area museum services in the UK. They vary in the way they operate, but generally are a source of advice, subsidise conservation work, make grants of up to 50% for improvements in museum facilities, and may provide a forum for museums in the area through training courses and meetings.

The Museums Association

The Museums Association is the national body bringing together museums as institutions and those working in them. The monthly Museums Bulletin is the newspaper of the museum world. The Museums Association also publishes quarterly the Museums Journal and an annual yearbook. It holds an annual conference, at which there is a commercial exhibition from manufacturers of goods relevant to museums, for example display systems and printing.
The Museums Association, 34 Bloomsbury Way,
London WC1A 2SF.

The Association of Independent Museums

A membership organisation for museums and galleries not administered directly or indirectly, by central or local government. AIM has its own Bulletin and organises regular seminars and meetings for its members.

AIM, c/o Michael Ware, National Motor Museum, Beaulieu, Hants SO4 7ZN.

Historic Houses Association

An association of owners and guardians of historic houses, parks and gardens. It acts as a spokesman for their interests. The HHA publishes a quarterly magazine, 'Historic House'. It holds two trade shows each year, a Garden Fair in June and a Heritage Trade Fair in conjunction with its AGM in the autumn. The Historic Houses Association provides advice to members and holds seminars, and publishes occasional papers and manuals.

Historic Houses Association, 38 Ebury Street, London SW1W 0LU.

Museum Stores Association of America

The professional body for those working in museum trading in the USA. Its annual conference, in May, provides interesting workshops, seminars and lectures, as well as an opportunity to meet those working in the field. These are trade shows held in conjunction with the annual conference. The MSA is regionalised and UK members are included in the North East Region. The MSA's journal 'MUST' is published quarterly.

Museum Stores Association of America, 61 South Pine Street, Doylestown, PA 18901, USA.

Charities Advisory Trust

A registered charity which helps charities and museums with their trading (and any other money-earning schemes). Hilary Blume, the author of this book, is the Director of the Trust. The Trust provides a special service to museums through its Museum Development Unit. It can advise on any aspect of museum trading, and can be retained on a consultancy basis. As well as advice, the Trust organises occasional seminars on various aspects of trading. It produces, on a non-profit basis in conjunction with museums, a range of goods, mainly cards, suitable for sale in museum shops.

Charities Advisory Trust, Radius Works, Back Lane, Hampstead, London NW3 1HL.

The Group for Museum Publishing and Shop Management

This is the specialist section within the Museums Association. Its members are all concerned with trading. The Group publishes an occasional newsletter and holds seminars. It organises an annual trade show at the Arts Council where museums can display their wares.

MUSPUB, Ian Charlton, Ashmolean Museum, Oxford.

Enterprise Agencies

These exist in most areas. They are designed to help small businesses. Staffed by managers on secondment from banking, industry and commerce they provide free advice on any business problem. The local telephone directory will give the address of your local Enterprise Agency.

Small Firms Service

This is a national, government provided service offering advice to small businesses. The Small Firms Service can be useful in helping to locate goods and services, for example a paper bag manufacturer. It publishes a range of basic booklets on running a business.

The local telephone directory will give the address of your local SFS.

The Booksellers Association

Membership of the Booksellers Association helps in opening accounts with the major book publishers and also allows one to take part in the selling and exchanging of book tokens. The Association also runs a range of training courses.

The Booksellers Association, 154 Buckingham Palace Road, London SW1W 9TZ.

Publications

The Department of Museum Studies, University of Leicester, 105 Princes Road East, Leicester produce an 89pp **Bibliography on Museum Studies Training**. (£3.45 including postage and packing.)

The South East Area Museum Service's publication **'The Local Museum: notes for amateur curators'** is a publication likely to be useful to anyone working in any museum, if only for its very comprehensive references.

'The Charity Trading Handbook' by Hilary Blume, Charities Advisory Trust, is the fullest account on the subject, and covers museum trading in part.

The Directory of Social Change, Radius Works, Back Lane, Hampstead, London NW3 1HL has the most comprehensive range of publications on fund-raising, public relations and financial management for non-profit organisations. The most relevant ones are:

> **The Guide to Company Giving**
> **A Guide to the Major Grant Making Trusts**
> **Raising Money from Industry**
> **Industrial Sponsorship and Joint Promotions**
> **Marketing: a guide for charities**
> **Accounting and Financial Management**
> **Raising Money for the Arts (new edition due)**

Books on business studies are relevant to the museum trader, and certainly offer a different perspective on the whole operation. The **Pan Breakthrough** series on business management provides a good introduction, as do many of the titles in **the Pelican Business and Management** range.

The Association of Independent Museums have a range of relevant publications. Contact them for a full list. Amongst them are:

> F R Veal: **Museum Public Relations**
> Valerie Shepard: **Reproduction fees**, photography etc: guidelines for museums
> **Museum Security** (AIM sheet no. 25)
> **Fund-raising for Museums** (AIM guidelines 4)

Insurance for Independent Museums (AIM guidelines 7)
Publishing Guidebooks and Postcards (AIM Information Paper 1)

Also useful are

Employment Practice and Law for the Independent Museum (AIM)

Sheila Durowska: **Employing people in voluntary organisations** (Bedford Square Press)

How to form a Friends Society for your Local Museum or Art Gallery £3.00 from Mrs R Marsh, 66 The Downs, Altrincham, Cheshire WA14 2QJ.

Marketing for small publishers (Interaction)

Arthur Andersen & Co.: **Business Sponsorship of the Arts – a Guide** (ABSA)

Henry Lydiate: **Visual Artists Copyright** (Artlaw)

Charles Gibbs-Smith: **Copyright law concerning works of art, photographs, and the written and spoken word** (Museums Association Information sheet)

The Commercial Use of Photographic Collections (AIM Information Paper 5)

Thomas H. Aageson: **Financial Analysis for Museum Stores** Museum Stores Association $20; available from Museum Stores Association, 61 South Pine Street, Doylestown, PA 18901.
A marvellous source of hard information on museum trading.

Newsletters targeted to museums, historic houses, cathedrals, etc

MUSPUB – Group for Museum Publishing and Shop Management.
Periodic newsletter available to members (contact Ian Charlton, Ashmolean Museum, Oxford).
AIM – Association of Independent Museums
AIM Bulletin (bi-monthly) sent to members. Editor: Diana Zeuner, Park Cottage, West Dean, Chichester, West Sussex.

163

Cathedral News – a very basic duplicated newsletter distributed to cathedrals and churches with bookstalls.

A. Guy Taylor, 11 Thorpe Chase, Ripon, North Yorkshire HG4 1VA.

Historic Houses Association – **Historic House** – journal of the Historic Houses Association circulated to members. HHA, Ebury Street, London SW1.

Museum Bulletin and **Museums Association Journal** – 34 Bloomsbury Way, London WC1.

Museum Stores Association of America – **MUST** – quarterly journal – available to members. Individual copies carry a cover price of $5. 61 South Pine Street, Doylestown, PA 18901, USA.

General newsletters which may be of interest to those in museum trading

The Bookseller – weekly – can be ordered through newsagents. Lists and reviews new publications.

Profitable Greetings – a free magazine supplied to those involved in the gift card trade. Quadrant House, The Quadrant, Sutton, Surrey.

BPMA News – free newspaper about promotional and incentive merchandise. British Promotional Merchandise Association, Osborn House, 21–25 Lower Stone Street, Maidstone, Kent.

Museum News – the journal of National Heritage, the museum action group. Deals with issues of interest in museums, including trading. 9a North Street, London SW4 0HN.

Funding sources

The best publications on fund-raising can be traced through the booklist provided by the educational charity, **the Directory of Social Change**, Radius Works, Back Lane, Hampstead, London NW3 1HL (tel: 01–435 8171). Many of these, for example The Guide to Company Giving, Raising Money from Trusts, and Raising Money for the Arts, will be of particular use.

The Directory of Social Change also provides a range of training courses and seminars on fund-raising – write and ask to be notified.

The National Council of Voluntary Organisations produce a 'Selective Bibliography of fund-raising books and pamphlets'; NCVO, 26 Bedford Square, London WC1B 3HU.

Your Area Museum Service may offer advice on fund-raising, and can give grants of up to 50% for museum improvements.

The Association for Business Sponsorship of the Arts, 2 Chester Street, London SW1X 7BB, helps promote business sponsorship. It also keeps a register of organisations seeking support, so you can register any particular project with them. Also, the Office of Arts and Libraries, through its **Business Sponsorship Incentive Scheme**, undertakes to match the amounts raised by new business sponsorship. Full details can be obtained from ABSA, 2 Chester Street, London SW1.

The **regional tourist boards** are empowered to make grants towards the capital costs of projects aimed towards the development of tourism. By combining the museum shop with a tourist information centre, museums may be eligible for grants for constructing, or adapting, their museum shops. These may also qualify for grants for the running costs of the tourist information centre from their local authority. Contact your regional tourist board, and talk to the local authority.
Consult their leaflet: Financing Tourist Projects (English Tourist Board).

The Charities Aid Foundation, 48 Pembury Road, Tonbridge, Kent, produce the Directory of Grant Making Trusts at a daunting £45, which lists all major trusts.

The Museums and Galleries Commission can offer grants for building works in museums; Museums and Galleries Commission, 2 Carlton Gardens, London SW1.

Training

Training is provided through occasional seminars by Muspub; AIM; the Directory of Social Change; the Booksellers' Association; Area Museum Services; the Historic Houses Association; and the

Charities Advisory Trust. (See under 'Organisations which can help' and 'Funding'.)

The PIRA (Printing Industries Research Association) organises courses on printing; PIRA, Randalls Road, Leatherhead, Surrey (tel: 0372 376161).

The London School of Publishing, 47 Red Lion Street, London WC1R 4PF (tel: 01–405 9801) has courses on all aspects of publishing.

Trade Fairs

The main UK Gift Fair is **the Spring Fair**, National Exhibition Centre, Birmingham, held during the first week in February (Sunday to Thursday).

Harrogate Gift Fair, July.

Top Drawer in London (this year at the Kensington Exhibition Centre); 250 exhibitors of 'up-market' gift ware and stationery.
Organiser: Dresswell Exhibitions, 27 Queensdale Place, Holland Park, London W11 (tel: 01–727 1929).

Souvenir Show; end of October, in London. About fifty of the major souvenir manufacturers. A place to find pens, bookmarks, pencils, key fobs, postcards, tea towels, should you want to!
Organiser: Pressex Promotions, Osborn House, 21–25 Lower Stone Street, Maidstone, Kent.

Muspub; Arts Council, in April.

Booksellers Association Trade Exhibition; Metropole Hotel, Brighton – one day in May. Two-thirds of exhibitors are publishers, but also exhibiting are shop display systems, security systems and design and printing services.

Publishing Services Exhibition and Print Buying Exhibition; July, in London.

Museums visited as part of the project on museum trading

Abbeydale Industrial Hamlet, Sheffield

Abergavenny and District Museum

Acton Scott Working Farm Museum, Shropshire

American Museum in Britain, Bath

Ashmolean Museum of Art and Archaeology, Oxford

Avoncroft Museum of Buildings

Bethnal Green Museum of Childhood

Birmingham Museum and Art Gallery

Blackburn Museum and Art Gallery

Blists Hill Open Air Museum, Telford

Boat Museum, Ellesmere Port

Brighton Museum and Art Gallery

Bristol Museum and Art Gallery

British Library

British Museum

British Museum (Natural History), London

Bronte Parsonage Museum, Haworth

Burgh House, Hampstead

Burnley Museum and Art Gallery

Buttercross Museum, Ludlow

Cambridge and County Folk Museum

Castle Museum, York

Cecil Higgins Art Gallery, Bedford

Christchurch Library, Oxford

Christchurch Mansion, Ipswich

Church Farm House Museum, London

Churchill Gardens Museum, Hereford

Coalbrookdale Museum, Telford

Coalport Museum, Telford

Colmans Mustard Museum, Norwich

Corinium Museum Cirencester

Courtauld Institute Galleries

Dickens House, London

Dyson Perrins Museum of Worcester Porcelain

E. Lancs Regiment Museum, Blackburn

Ferens Art Gallery, Hull

Fitzwilliam Museum, Cambridge

Geffrye Museum, London

Geological Museum, London

Glasgow Art Gallery and Museums

Gloucester City Museum and Gallery

Graves Art Gallery, Sheffield

The Guildhall Library, London

Ham House, London

Hampton Court Palace

Harris Museum and Art Gallery, Preston

Heptonstall Old Grammar School, Hebden Bridge

Hereford City Museum and Art Gallery

Holburne of Menstrie Museum, Bath

Horniman Museum

Imperial War Museum

Industrial Museum, Bradford

Ipswich Museum

Ironbridge Gorge Museum

Jewish Museum, London

Jorvik Viking Centre, York

Keats House, Hampstead

Kenwood, Hampstead

Lady Lever Art Gallery, Port Sunlight

Lavenham Guildhall

Leighton House Art Gallery and Museum

Lincoln City and County Museum

Liverpool County Museum

Llandrindod Museum, Llandrindod Wells

London Transport Museum

Manchester City Art Gallery

Mappin Art Gallery, Sheffield
Maritime Museum, Liverpool
Monmouth Museum
Museum of Canterbury
Museum of Cider, Hereford
Museum of London
Museum of Mankind, London
Museum of Modern Art, Oxford
Museum of Rural Life, Gloucester
National Army Museum
National Gallery
National Maritime Museum, Greenwich
National Museum of Labour History
National Museum of Wales
National Portrait Gallery
National Railway Museum, York
Norwich Castle Museum

Nottingham Castle Museum
Oxfordshire County Museum, Woodstock
Piece Hall, Halifax
Quarry Bank Mill, Styal
Robert Opie Collection
Royal Academy of Arts
Royal Pavilion, Brighton
Ruskin Gallery, Sheffield
Science Museum
Tate Gallery
Town Docks Museum, Hull
Ulster Museum, Belfast
Usher Gallery, Lincoln
Victoria & Albert Museum
Walker Art Gallery, Liverpool
Worcester City Museum
York City Art Gallery